A TRAIL OF HOPE

STORIES OF A SECOND CHANCE IN BAKER CITY

Published in Beaverton, Oregon, by Good Catch Publishing.
www.goodcatchpublishing.com
V1.1

Printed in the United States of America

TABLE OF CONTENTS

ACKNOWLEDGEMENTS

I would like to thank Brad Phillips for his vision for this book and for his hard work in making it a reality. To the people of Harvest, thank you for your boldness and vulnerability in sharing your personal stories.

This book would not have been published without the amazing efforts of our project manager and editor, Marie Osborne. Her untiring resolve pushed this project forward and turned it into a stunning victory. Thank you for your great fortitude and diligence.

Deep thanks to our incredible editor in chief, Michelle Cuthrell, and executive editor, Jen Genovesi, for all the amazing work they do. I would also like to thank our invaluable proofreader, Melody Davis, for the focus and energy she has put into perfecting our words.

Lastly, I want to extend our gratitude to the creative and very talented Jenny Randle, who designed the beautiful cover for *A Trail of Hope: Stories of a Second Chance in Baker City.*

Daren Lindley
President and CEO
Good Catch Publishing

The book you are about to read
is a compilation of authentic life stories.
The facts are true, and the events are real.
These storytellers have dealt with crisis, tragedy, abuse
and neglect and have shared their most private moments,
mess-ups and hang-ups in order for others to learn and
grow from them. In order to protect the identities of those
involved in their pasts, the names and details of some
storytellers have been withheld or changed.

INTRODUCTION

What do you do when life is careening out of control? When addiction overtakes you or abuse chains you with fear? Is depression escapable? Will relationships ever be healthy again? Are we destined to dissolve into an abyss of sorrow? Or will the sunlight of happiness ever return?

Your life really can change. It is possible to become a new person. The six stories you are about to read prove positively that people right here in our town have stopped dying and started living. Whether you've been beaten by abuse, broken promises, shattered dreams or suffocating addictions, the resounding answer is, "Yes! You can become a new person." The potential to break free from gloom and into a bright future awaits.

Expect inspiration, hope and transformation! As you walk with these real people from our very own city through the pages of this book, you will not only find riveting accounts of their hardships, you will learn the secrets that brought about their breakthroughs. These people are no longer living in the shadows of yesterday; they are thriving with a sense of mission and purpose TODAY. May these stories inspire you to do the same.

A REBELLIOUS SON
THE STORY OF ANTHONY
WRITTEN BY AMEERAH COLLINS

I cowered in a corner of the bed. My breathing quickened, and my heartbeat thundered in my chest. My sweaty palms shook as I clutched at my throbbing skull and tangled hair. I clenched my eyes shut and banged my head against the headboard, desperately willing away the feelings of paranoia and dread. None of this was real, and I knew that — but the fear *was* real and seeped so deep in my veins that every limb of my body trembled.

Stop it! It's just another trip, Anthony. Monsters aren't real! None of this is real. It's all just a figment of your imagination. It's just the meth, man — it's just the meth.

Or was it? Though I told myself it was all make believe, I didn't understand why I could hear the phantoms so well. I'd never had a trip last so long or be so vivid. It boggled my mind. They whispered to one another and talked so fast I couldn't catch a clear word between their dark hisses. I felt them inching closer to my spot on the bed, invading my space and driving me insane. I wanted to cry and shout, hoping someone in the house would hear me, bust my door down and save me from the wicked creatures in my room.

"Anthony," one voice hissed like a cunning predator, his voice deep, scratchy, impossibly low and drawing out my name, silencing me completely. It sounded wicked and evil, like something from a horror film. His voice beat upon my eardrums and slowly crept deep within my mind. "Come with us. Your time is up. Come with us, Anthony."

My body shuddered at the voice. Warm, moist breath abruptly blew upon my ear, as if someone had cupped his hands around his mouth and breathed straight into my ear. My shoulders shook.

I could feel a wretched wail rumbling in the pit of my gut, dying to be released, but not even a whimper crawled its way up my throat. I tried to calm myself. *It's just the drugs. It's just a bad trip.* But in my heart, I feared the truth might be something worse. No drug had ever conjured hellish creatures. No drug had ever left me feeling simultaneously damned, lost and confused.

Was this real after all? Was it punishment? *Was I finally going to hell?* I wondered — until I opened my eyes and knew I was already there.

ॐॐॐ

At just 3 years old, I was placed in foster care. Though I don't remember any of it, I was told my biological mother was married to a man who'd been caught molesting my brother Devan. Deemed unfit, we were promptly snatched from my mother.

My biological father had no qualms taking Devan in, but he didn't claim me as his own flesh and blood.

Therefore, he refused to accept custody of me. After a year of being shifted through various foster homes, I ended up with the Johnson family, and they adopted me. They loved me, and that was all that mattered to me.

Growing up, my 11 siblings and I were raised in a strict household with solid values. My dad was a pastor and my mother the leading woman of the church. There were a lot of us, so Dad had a firm hand for discipline, and it scared the heck out of us. Getting in trouble and facing his looks of disappointment and frustration, plus the spankings and groundings, was something I never wanted to encounter. My mother was kind with a heart of gold. However, as I grew older and reached my preteen years, my curiosity piqued. I suddenly became a stereotypical pastor's kid — a kid who knew right from wrong, but was just dying to get a taste of that oh-so-wicked world his parents spoke against.

At age 12, I smoked my first cigarette. I snuck into my neighbor's truck, stole his pack of cigarettes and lit up outside my house. The experience was horrible. I coughed and sputtered. It tasted bitter and awful. My oldest brother caught me, and he immediately told our dad. Dad ended up making me eat the rest of the cigarette, then walk over to the neighbor's house and apologize for stealing it.

At 14, I tried marijuana. I'd been riding the school bus home, sitting back in my seat, minding my own business, braced for the usual bumpy ride. A kid my age approached me, held a brown rolled-up paper in his fingers and pushed it toward me.

"Hey, man, try this, and let me know what you think."

"What is it?" I asked with a raised eyebrow, dubious about what he suddenly wanted to thrust in my face considering we barely ever talked.

"Chill, man." He snickered at my confused expression. "It's just a blunt, bro. Light it up, take a puff and pass it back to me. We'll just go back and forth. Everyone's doing it."

I took the "blunt," as he called it, from his hand and inhaled. I could feel the pleasant burn in my lungs and the tingles rushing through my blood. I handed it back to him, and we smoked it all the way home. I was giddy and suddenly knew what it was like to "have the munchies," but as soon as the bus stopped on my street, I ran home and locked myself in my room. I stretched across my bed, smelling the weed all over me and hoping my dad didn't bust me. Considering his rage over a cigarette, I knew he'd blow a gasket over me smoking weed. Once my high faded, I showered and eased out of my room, trying to play it cool and not give myself away. It worked. My parents and siblings never suspected a thing.

But after those puffs on the school bus, I was hooked. I enjoyed the feeling of being high, the increase in my senses, the dizzying effects, the giddy and happy feelings, the earthy and herbal smell — all of it kept me going back for more.

Getting high marked the start of my rebellion against everything my parents taught me.

When I was 15, I got in contact with my biological

brother, Devan. I wanted to visit him, but my parents refused. They said they had a bad feeling about sparking up relations with members of my biological family and warned me against it. I sought him out, anyway.

Devan was different from my brothers back home. He was into hardcore drugs — marijuana was insignificant to him. He cooked meth and used it, too. Devan didn't pressure me into doing meth, but something about his lifestyle appealed to me, and before I knew it, I couldn't get enough.

Meth got me higher than marijuana ever did, and the high was different. It wasn't the classic dizzy, hungry, hoot and holler sort of high. With this high, my confidence soared, and my energy skyrocketed. Though I knew it was wrong and my parents would have had my head for even thinking about trying meth, I didn't care. I enjoyed it, so I kept doing it. Eventually, I got into trying other drugs just for kicks. Cocaine, prescription meds, ecstasy — I wanted it all.

❧❧❧

A few years later, I traveled to Seattle to visit my uncle Damon and cousins. On my way there, I met a guy in Salt Lake City who sold drugs. It didn't take me long to find another stranger into drugs like me.

Years of hardcore drug use had transformed me into a pretty unsavory character, and gravitating toward another one was like second nature. I bought a bunch of meth off him, desperately seeking a good high. I swallowed it all down my throat. It was rough and even stung a bit, but I didn't care. I just wanted to reach the clouds. By the time I made it to Seattle, I felt extremely paranoid and feared people were after me.

I felt exposed in the brightly lit, dome-like bus station, increasing my paranoia. While waiting for my uncle, I desperately sought a hiding place in various secluded areas and behind unsuspecting strangers. Their yelps and pushes didn't faze me as I tugged one stranger after another in front of me. I kept thinking cops or FBI agents were coming to take me away.

I continued darting through the crowd, seeking a place to hide. When I spotted a large soda machine, my heart soared in crazed relief. I squeezed into the small gap behind the soda machine and waited for my uncle. I bit my lip until it became raw, rubbed at my skin and kept peeping out from behind the soda machine to make sure I hadn't missed my uncle.

Finally, Uncle Damon pulled up. I scurried from behind the soda machine, ran to his car, threw my suitcase in the backseat and hopped in. I hurriedly clasped my seatbelt and tapped my fingers against my knees. I slumped low in my seat, peering out the window and sinking even lower when I thought I saw an FBI agent.

"What's wrong with you, boy?" Uncle Damon looked at me with narrowed eyebrows and a scrunched nose. He was a strong, burly man, just like Dad.

He eyed me with a skeptical glint in his eyes — the

same glint Dad got when he knew I'd done something wrong.

"Nothing, nothing. I'm just happy to be here," I said with a hesitant grin. I tried to discreetly look over my shoulder and make sure cops weren't running toward our car, but I'm sure my uncle caught my paranoid look. "Can we just go? I want to see everyone. Please? I just want to get out of here."

When we arrived at Uncle Damon's house, I still felt like people were after me. Though I mingled and talked with my cousins, I just couldn't shake the feelings of suspicion. Even though I was safely inside the house with family surrounding me, I still didn't feel safe.

Later that night, I stepped onto the front porch for a breather, but suddenly found myself facing a group of Ku Klux Klan members draped in white robes with the pointed hoods. They carried flaming torches and nooses. They stood in my uncle's yard shouting obscenities and racial slurs, threatening to hang and kill my family.

"What are you doing? Get the h*** off my family's lawn, you racist freaks!" I screamed as they continued to call my family horrible names. I searched the porch for a weapon as they stepped closer to the house. I snagged a shovel and hopped down the steps of the porch and wildly swung it at them. "Get away from my family, or I'll kill you! I'll kill you all!"

"Anthony!" I could hear my uncle's frantic yet booming voice behind me, but I didn't want him to come any closer. "Put the shovel down, son. What are you doing out here?" Uncle Damon attempted to snatch the shovel from me, desperately trying to avoid my hard swings, but I simply pushed him away. He stumbled with widened eyes, surprised at my force.

"Get back in the house," I screamed at my uncle. "Don't just stand there — you need to go back inside. I won't let the KKK hurt you or the others."

I released a string of curses as I continued whipping the shovel through the air, but I was getting more and more frustrated when I was unable to strike any of the cloaked men.

"I'll kill you all before you lay a hand on my family. Come closer, I *dare* you. I'LL MURDER YOU!"

My uncle quickly ripped the shovel from my hands and tossed it across the yard.

"What did you do that for?" I shouted in shock. "Are you crazy? They're trying to kill you. I need to protect you guys."

"ANTHONY!" Uncle Damon hollered one last time. "Look at me. There is nobody there. There is no KKK in front of the house." He suddenly pulled me into a hug and tucked my head in his large shoulder as I tussled with him, struggling to let go. "For Pete's sake, kid. What did you take?"

I didn't respond as my uncle began to pray. He prayed for my hallucinations to cease and that God would give me the sense to stop abusing whatever drug I was using. Uncle Damon led me into the house, telling me not to look back at the front yard but to just go upstairs to my room. He prayed for me through the night, and after a while, I no longer heard the Ku Klux Klan raging outside the house.

When I woke up the following day, I thought the hallucinations were over. I felt fine, and I no longer had the high sensations that meth usually gave me. I ended up going to do some handiwork with my uncle's friend in a residential area. There were no porta-potties there, and I definitely wasn't going to knock on someone's door and weirdly ask to use his bathroom. So I went to a slightly wooded area to relieve my bladder. However, when I turned around I saw one of the residents, a creepy-looking older man, standing on his back balcony videotaping me pee. I freaked out, cursing and yelling at the man for his obscene behavior before he abruptly vanished into thin air. That's when I knew the hallucinations were still happening.

As the day dragged on, I again began fearing the cops were after me. It was worse than how I felt at the bus station the day before. This time, the cops were getting closer and closer, and I had nowhere to run or hide. My uncle's friend became so concerned for my wellbeing, and his own safety, that he drove me back home to Uncle Damon.

Uncle Damon prayed with me for a while, but he soon left me in my room to hit the sack. I sat there pondering to myself. I had no idea why I was still tripping from my last meth usage. I didn't understand why it was taking such an extreme toll on me. I knew I ate it instead of snorting or shooting it, but I didn't know that would have such an adverse effect on me.

While sitting against the headboard, I thought about my parents and siblings back home. I knew they would have a conniption if they could see the position I was in. The Bible-based principles and scriptures my father preached about on Sunday mornings and the many talks my parents had with me and my siblings regarding God filtered through my mind.

I shook my head and released a humorless chuckle full of strain and disbelief. "What if God came back right this second? I'd go straight to hell."

With those thoughts in my head, I lay down with my eyes closed, willing the hallucinations to be over by the morning.

When I could feel myself drifting off to sleep, I abruptly heard a soft thumping and whispering in my room. It started off low and breathy, barely even there. I figured I was having another hallucination, so I tried to ignore it. The voices became louder as they spoke to one another. Such sinister talk put me on edge and made me realize this hallucination was a wicked one.

I eased myself into a corner of the bed, trembling and shaking as I could practically feel the evilness those voices oozed resting upon my skin. Rationally, I knew this was because of the drugs. However, part of me felt like the devil was using my horrible state to his advantage. That he knew I'd grown up as a pastor's kid — a kid who knew right from wrong, but wanted to play around with the wrong. In that moment, I felt like the devil himself was trying to scare the hell out of me. And when I opened my eyes and saw the monsters in my room, I truly believed them to be straight from hell.

Several of them surrounded my bed, at least five or six. They resembled huge ogres with long arms, fanged mouths, crooked legs and wide nostrils. They had muscular bodies, stringy hair and grim faces with long scratches across their sunken eyes and paper-thin lips. Their sharp teeth dripped thick, dark and murky blood, which trickled down their stout jaws and thick necks. Some had scaly skin as dark as coal, while others appeared gray and ashy.

The biggest one stood at the foot of the bed, his head nearly touching the ceiling. He grew horns from his forehead, and a devious glint was in his eyes.

He grinned at me, a cruel and sick leer. He outstretched his large and clawed hands toward me, and somewhere deep inside, I felt certain this was Satan, come to take me away.

"Anthony," he sneered my name. "It's time to go to hell." He threw his head back and laughed as I attempted to scream and shout. "Oh, come on now, Anthony. You knew this was coming. You've been on my turf for a while. Now you've got hell to pay."

More demonic creatures suddenly appeared. They crawled from under the bed and magically leapt through the walls and landed inches from me. I bolted from the bed and ran out of the room and down the hall. They chased me through the house as I screamed for my uncle. I stumbled and raced down the stairs as the creatures thumped behind me, their heavy feet pounding across the wooden floor. I finally reached the front door and ran outside, but they were out there, too. They jumped from the woods, led by the one I took to be Satan, intent on dragging me to hell.

"NO! NO! I DON'T WANT TO GO TO HELL! GOD! HELP ME!" I screamed before a large body suddenly grabbed me from behind and turned me into a massive hug. I tussled with the body before I recognized Uncle Damon's voice screaming the name of Jesus.

"Get back, Satan! In the name of Jesus, loose your hold on him!" Uncle Damon roared in front of me. Though I'd thought the creatures in my room had strong and powerful bellowing voices, my uncle's voice was stronger. I felt the godly strength radiating from his tone, and it vibrated through his chest.

I wept in Uncle Damon's arms as he prayed for me that night. The torturous screams of the demonic creatures slowly faded away as my uncle half-carried me inside. My feet slumped and dragged against the floor as I clutched onto him, terrified that I would be dragged to hell if I let go at all. He pulled me into my room and prayed for me until I drifted off to sleep.

The following night, I had my last hallucination. I thought someone was trying to steal my uncle's car. As I yelled and screamed out the window, trying to scare the person off, Uncle Damon walked up beside me again and told me I was hallucinating. After he prayed for me, I fell asleep. It was almost like every time my hallucinations got out of hand, Uncle Damon would pray for me, and God would put me right to sleep. That amazed me.

The following few days, I didn't experience any more hallucinations, however, I had a new perspective on God. I knew the meth caused the hallucinations, but in my heart I truly believed those monstrous creatures were, in fact, hellish demons. I believed the devil tried to scare me so badly because he wanted me to lose my mind. In church, I'd heard people talk about how the devil oftentimes tried to steal the minds of youngsters, but I didn't really understand until I felt like he attempted to take mine.

However, I also believed that God intervened through the devil's tactics by keeping Uncle Damon by my side. I could have had those horrible trips at some random party or club where people would have simply laughed and mocked me. They undoubtedly would have called the cops on me if I did something too crazy, and who knows what else would have happened considering the illegal drugs in my system. But it happened at my uncle's house — an uncle who happened to be a preacher with an intense love for God.

I believed God was telling me, *Enough is enough.* It was time to push drugs aside and bring God to the center. Time to go back to my childhood teachings and remember what my parents taught me about staying close to God, reading my Bible and keeping myself away from the wrong crowd. But even though I felt like God was speaking this to me, I didn't listen. Those horrible trips weren't enough to send me crying back to church.

I was too in love with the high to change my ways.

❧ ❧ ❧

In my early 20s, all I wanted to do was get high, drink alcohol and sleep around. Though it may seem crazy, I always prayed to God that he wouldn't allow me to get a girl pregnant unless she was supposed to be my wife.

And though I was still haunted by the creatures I'd encountered on my meth-induced trip three years prior, I still couldn't shake the all-consuming desire for that one perfect high. Maybe it would be the next trip or the next drug, but I was driven to find it and feel that indescribable rush.

One night near the beginning of the summer, my buddy Rod and I were hanging out at his "baby momma's" house when we decided to hit up his dealer and buy some ecstasy. Though we just wanted to try it, we ended up buying 24 pills, 12 for each of us. They were double stacked with MDMA and laced with meth. I hadn't used meth in quite a while, so when we chopped the pills up and snorted them, the effect was instantaneous. My energy erupted like a volcanic blast of euphoria, an explosive rush.

When we settled into our high, we simply sat on the living room sofa. Rod was on my right, but when I glanced to my left, I noticed our friend Tristan sitting beside me. I struck up an in-depth conversation with him, while Rod laughed his head off. I turned to him and grinned at his hunched-over position, waiting for him to announce what was so funny.

"Bro," Rod said between fits of laughter, "who are you talking to?"

I chuckled, deeming him dense. "Dude, I'm talking to Tristan. He's right here. I didn't see him come in, but he's here!"

"There's nobody there, Anthony! Tristan is not here, man." He continued to laugh at my expense as I turned back to Tristan, but he was gone.

Later that night, we had an urge to smoke, and we ended up driving to a friend's house to get some weed. Although much of the night remains a big blur, and I can't remember what all happened, I do know that Rod and I were stoned beyond belief. The following day, we talked to our friend who'd supplied us the weed, and he said that Rod and I were so high he had no idea how we were functioning, much less driving. He'd never seen anyone so high on ecstasy before. When he said that, a slight shiver skittered up my spine. Even though I hadn't heeded God's warning three years before, I believed he was still looking out for me.

I hated how undeserving I was of his protection, but I thanked him for having his hand on my life, anyway.

That summer, I tried a few more drugs here and there. There would be times that Rod, Tristan and I would be so high that our entire reality would completely shift. One night we took acid and decided to play *Call of Duty.* We ended up seeing the characters in the game as a bunch of Lego men instead of computerized soldiers. Later that night, we stretched out on the grass and gazed at the stars twinkling across the midnight sky.

We lay there in complete awe and silence as the stars smoothed down, then cramped back up. They were like wavy patterns that greatly intrigued us. After a strange high that lasted more than six hours, I decided acid wasn't for me. It was just too weird.

ॐ ॐ ॐ

Halloween night, I attended a costume party in an apartment complex. The pungent mixture of smoke, sweat and alcohol filled my nostrils. I leaned against a wall, feeling slightly suffocated by all the loud voices, gyrating bodies and piercing hip-hop music when I saw her walk through the door. She appeared out of her element, as if she didn't even want to be there. All I could concentrate on was her beauty and talking myself into approaching her. Soon after, I pushed my way through the crowd and made my way over to her.

"Hey." My voice was slurred and slightly sluggish — I was high and a little drunk. "I'm Anthony. I noticed you walk in a while ago. What's your name?"

"Christelle," she replied with a raised eyebrow. She folded her arms as she eyed me apprehensively, waiting for me to speak. "Do you need anything?"

"It's really nice to meet you," I said. I don't know why,

but I was a nervous wreck. It may have been the drugs and alcohol getting to me, but I repeated that same sentence to her at least 15 times. She looked at me as if I was crazy. "I'm sorry, I'm just … I'm nervous. And it's just really nice to meet you."

"Yeah, I know." Christelle chuckled. "So, it's Anthony, right? How old are you? You look super young. You can't possibly be old enough to be as stoned and wasted as you are. You have any ID on you, kid?"

"I'm 23! I'm pretty sure I'm older than you!" I laughed while digging my wallet from my back pocket.

"Oh, please. No, you're not."

"Fine," I playfully grumbled. "If you insist on carding me, by all means, see for yourself."

After my jitters finally subsided and Christelle checked my license for my age, we ended up spending the entire night together. My friends, being the knuckleheads that they were, decided it would be funny to handcuff us together because we were hitting it off so well. But it didn't matter if we were handcuffed together or not, for the next two weeks Christelle and I spent nearly every waking moment together. The only dreadful times we had to force ourselves to separate were when she had to attend her college classes.

The next month, Christelle discovered she was pregnant. After she spent Thanksgiving in Oregon with her family, we decided to tell her parents about the pregnancy. We were pretty nervous and even slightly scared because I had never met her parents, and like me,

Christelle had grown up in a conservative, church-centered household. Breaking news to our parents of a pregnancy before marriage was pretty nail-biting.

Christelle and I arrived at her house when her mother, Mrs. Braxton, was at home, but her father was still at work. We sat in the dining room, Mrs. Braxton and me, getting to know one another. Her mom finally stood up, and Christelle followed after her.

"Mom." Christelle stood beside my chair and fidgeted with her hands before firmly clasping them behind her back. "I get the house."

Her mom cocked her head to the side in confusion before asking, "Christelle, what in the world are you talking about?"

"Um." Christelle sighed, unclasped her hands and began to wring them before shrugging with her palms faced up. "Remember when you said to Drake and me that whoever gives you and Dad grandkids first gets the house? Well, looks like I beat my brother." She softly chuckled. "I get the house, Mom."

Christelle's pregnancy finally registered with her mom, and she began to cry as she reached out toward Christelle and pulled her into a hug. "We're going to have to tell your father," her mom said. "It may be a little hard to adjust, but it'll be okay."

"Thanks, Mom." Christelle laid her head on her mother's shoulder and cried with her before suddenly lifting her head and saying, "Oh, and Anthony's the father!"

"Yeah, Christelle, I figured." Mrs. Braxton grinned through her tears.

When Christelle's father returned home from work, we had a really serious discussion regarding our future with the baby. We all sat at the dining room table. Christelle and I sat on one side, and her parents sat on the other. I could feel the doubt and slight frustration in her father's eyes, but I was determined to assure him of my ability to care for his daughter and grandchild.

"So what are you guys going to do?" he asked as he tried to rub the worried creases out of his forehead. "You still have to finish school, Christelle. And from what your mother tells me, Anthony here doesn't have a steady job or a true means to take care of you and the baby. Do you two have a plan or …"

"I'm going to grow up, Mr. Braxton. I know it may be difficult for you to believe right now considering my situation and this unplanned pregnancy and all, but I'm going to get a steady job and take care of Christelle and my kid."

"That's not as easy as it sounds, Anthony. There's a lot of work, pressure and responsibility involved in raising a child, especially when you two are already so young. I'm just worried about my little girl."

I knew Christelle's parents didn't believe a word I was saying about growing up and getting a job to take care of my family, but I was determined to show them how wrong they were about me.

For a while there, it didn't look good. Christelle moved

back to Oregon to live with her parents, and I stayed in Seattle to work. I'm sure it seemed to her parents like I wasn't keeping up my end of the bargain, but staying in Seattle was part of the plan. I was trying to make enough money to get my own place in Oregon, so that I could be with Christelle and our child.

A couple months later, I moved to Baker City and landed a good job. Christelle and I were in a committed relationship, but I noticed that while we were apart she'd made some drastic changes in her life. While I had cut back on my hardcore drug usage and mostly limited myself to smoking marijuana, Christelle had returned to church and was trying to live her life for God.

"There are just certain things I don't want to do anymore, you know?" Christelle told me one evening. "I pray a lot, Anthony. I want to be the sort of woman my parents raised me to be. I want to mold my heart with the love of Jesus." She sighed with pure bliss. "Partying, getting wasted and pushing God to the sidelines — that's not me anymore. I can feel God again, and all I want to do is please him."

I chuckled to myself and reached my hand toward Christelle's slightly protruding belly. Though I didn't feel any kicks, I knew our little Logan was in there. I felt like he was just waiting for me to grow up and get it right like Christelle had in my absence.

"I get it, Christelle. I may have rebelled and all, but I'm still a pastor's kid. I've always known the way to God. He's always stayed on my mind and in my heart, even when I was in the streets doing whatever," I sincerely told her. "And, heck, you and Logan make me want to reevaluate my own life."

Christelle slyly grinned and shrugged. "Who knows? Maybe you should."

Soon after, I really began to reflect on my life. I thought about my awesome mom and dad and how even though I'd fled the church and did plenty of things that surely displeased God, their teachings never left me. Even in my drug-related stupors and intoxicated moments, I still took the time to thank God and think about him simply because my parents laid that foundation in me. Why did God love me so much that he allowed such a great family to adopt me?

I thought about Uncle Damon and how God allowed him to take charge during my frightening hallucinations and help me overcome those hellish three days. Just seeing him pray to the God of the universe and see that same almighty God answer his prayers for me — how great was that? I wanted a connection with God like Uncle Damon had. I wanted my son to look up to me in times of need just like I'd looked to my uncle in my time of calamity. How could God have not given up on me in such a horrible and despicable time of my life?

Just going over my life and shaking my head at all the ludicrous decisions and mistakes I made, I recognized a deep desire in myself to live for Jesus and give my son a great father to look up to. I knew family and friends who'd lived the sort of lifestyle I lived, and they ended up in the grave or in prison. In that moment, I knew there was no way I was going to have Logan grow up and inform folks his father died from a drug overdose or was locked up for possession of illegal drugs. Heck, no! That wasn't going to be my kid.

I stopped doing drugs cold turkey. I didn't want nor did I feel the need to join a rehabilitation center or special program. I wanted to kick my drug habit, just me and God.

Throughout my withdrawals, the vomiting, the intense cravings and sickness, I relied on Jesus for my wellbeing. I constantly prayed and read my Bible, leaning on God and asking him to help me. I figured that if I trusted in God and became totally clean for him, then God would keep me clean. Though I wanted to get clean for Christelle, myself and Logan, I really wanted to do it for God. He had been there for me through all the hard times, and I was grateful for that. He never left me, even though I'd abandoned him.

While relying on prayer and willpower to stay away from drugs, I also disconnected myself from people who would talk to me about drugs or bring it in my presence. My entire circle of friends and acquaintances changed.

My next step was going to church. Although I'd accepted Jesus back into my heart and made the decision to live for him, I knew I needed to find a church, too. I grew up in church. I knew that being around others who shared a deep love for Christ was important in staying close to God. That sort of community atmosphere and familial support was significant to strengthening my love for, belief in and dedication to God.

When I walked into Harvest Church, I instantly felt an atmosphere of love. I'd missed singing songs of love to God and raising my hands to show my affection to him. I'd missed that feeling of togetherness. I felt like I was finally home, like being around God's people was the ultimate high I had spent years of my life searching for. I was the rebellious son who'd finally come home to his first love: God and his son, Jesus Christ.

Harvest was the church Christelle and her family belonged to. I didn't want the members to look down on me as just some guy who'd messed around with Christelle and gotten her pregnant. I wanted to be another brother coming to the church to show God his love. I wanted to be accepted. But I felt so guilty and ashamed for the life I'd lived. I could barely look anyone in the eye, and I felt like everyone could see every horrible thing I'd done or every dirty little secret my mind harbored. I couldn't have been more wrong about those people and how they perceived me.

As soon as I walked through those church doors, many of the people there had already accepted me. Pastor Phillips, the youth pastor at the time, pulled me to the side and asked to have coffee with me at a nearby coffee shop. We talked for hours that day, and I told him my life story, from before my adoption to my relocation to Baker City. I just spilled my guts right there on the table before him.

"I've never been there, Anthony," he said with a

solemn yet humble look. "Like you, I grew up a pastor's kid and had the love of God instilled in me from the very beginning. The only difference is that I didn't try certain things. I stayed in the church. But just because you didn't stay in church doesn't mean the church didn't stay in you."

I looked up at him and nodded my head in understanding. I was amazed at how well he knew what was going on in my mind and heart. How did he know throughout my years of wrongdoing that I continuously thought of God?

"The person you were months ago is not the person sitting across from me right now," he said, chuckling at my lopsided grin. "You've reopened your heart to God, and he's already changed you so much. This isn't an easy road you're on — getting sober for God, leaving your past behind and raising a family. But know that I love you. Harvest loves you. And most importantly, God loves you, and he's going to help you *and* Christelle along the way. All he asks is that you follow Jesus and live for him. Can you do that?"

"Yeah, of course," I said. "It's all I want to do."

❧❧❧

Christelle gave birth to Logan, and we married. Though he had a few complications at birth, God brought him through it all, and he is healthy. Since then, Christelle gave birth to our first little girl, Raven, and then two years later, Nina.

Just like our parents did with us, Christelle and I now strive to raise our children with a great foundation in Jesus Christ. As a sober man, I became able to channel that intense protective love of my family that once prompted me to swing out at phantoms with a shovel. I promised Christelle's parents I'd grow up and take care of her and our family, and that's what I've tried to do — encouraging my children not to learn the hard way like I did, but to stay with God throughout all their days and to never leave him.

SWEET SURRENDER
THE STORY OF KATIE
WRITTEN BY ARLENE SHOWALTER

"I can't do this anymore." My sobs echoed through the vacant room. I crept into the living room, also void of life. My sons' toys lay scattered like discarded leaves across the floor. I had no will or heart to pick up even one. Silence pummeled my ears as I made my way to the garage.

My bare feet shuffled across the cool concrete as I searched a specific corner. "Where is it?" I dug around the boxes, searching for the rifle. *Nothing.*

I retraced my steps and stepped over each toy like tiptoeing around sacred relics. My whole being ached as I climbed back into my empty king-sized bed and threw the covers over my head. "I can't even kill myself right."

৯৯৯

"You again." Annoyance tinged my voice at the junior grinning at me. I worked as a residential assistant in an Oregon college. A wide room and my office separated the girls' and boys' dorms.

"Hey, Katie."

I scowled at his broad grin.

"What's your excuse this time, Darius?" I asked, standing between him and the refuge of the boys' side.

He took two steps toward me, smile intact.

"Let's see. Last time your excuse was you were fixing a fridge in the girls' dorm. Fridge not working again?" I crossed my arms and waited.

"No. I was out walking and got lost." He crossed his heart with a single finger. "Promise."

"After curfew? You know I have to write you up. Again."

He loped into my office with easy grace, turned a chair backward and plopped down. He rested his elbow on the chair back and his chin in his cupped hand. "Do your duty, Miss Residential Assistant. You caught me."

I sat down and pulled the requisite form from my desk drawer. "Let's see if I can remember — Darius …"

"Darius Scott."

"Okay, Mr. Scott, what's your *official* excuse this time?"

Darius hung around long after I'd filled out the form and collected his signature. He spoke with the same ease he displayed trotting down the basketball court and scoring a three-pointer.

For the next two years, Darius hung out at my office, seeming to prefer my company to campus jocks. We discussed everything and nothing. I loved hiking and camping. Darius smiled in bored amusement. I disliked sports, indoor particularly, but attended all his games to watch him play.

Darius kept his emotions on an even keel — always.

He's so easy to be with, I thought, as we strolled

around campus, hand in hand. *So unlike Dad, who's always a ticking time bomb, ever ready to explode.*

One time I perched on the bleachers as the team played a home game. A collective groan rose from the crowd as a teammate missed a basket at the final buzzer, and we lost the game. His head and shoulders drooped as his teammates shunned him with their backs. Darius walked over, shook his hand and draped an arm across his shoulder. They walked side by side to the locker room.

I sat cemented to my seat as the grumbling crowd dissipated like mist on the Puget Sound. *Dad would slap me into next week if I'd missed that shot. Come to think of it, Dad didn't even need a reason to beat me bloody.* I thought of the time he'd flayed me with his belt. I forged a doctor's note so I wouldn't have to expose my flogged body in gym class.

Darius is everything Dad isn't. Patient, kind, polite.

We drifted into a sexual relationship. *Surely Darius is committed to me now.* But, as graduation approached, I could find no signs of him feeling or thinking that way. After commencement, he took a job in town, while I found a great job working on a youth ranch — and put five hours between us.

I guess I know where I stand with Darius. Obviously he doesn't love me enough to commit to anything, so I'll chalk it up to experience and get on with life.

❧❧❧

"Can I come see you?" Darius called me a few weeks later.

"Sure, but why?"

"I miss you."

"You can come if you want, but strictly as a *friend.*"

"I'm fine with that."

I rolled my eyes at his unflappable tone.

My newfound independence seemed to attract Darius, and he began inching toward a real relationship.

Meanwhile, I moved several times and ended up back with my parents.

Darius followed each move and managed to reengage my heart, but again he halted short of making a commitment to me and any future together.

"I'm really tired of this back and forth," I told him on one visit. I threw my hands up in the air.

"I can't continue to invest in a relationship that you clearly are not interested in pursuing. Either we're going forward, or I'm done."

A few days later, on New Year's Eve, Darius showed up at my job with a ring and the words I'd waited for years to hear. "I don't want to lose you."

Joy surged through me as I drove home, my eyes ping-ponging between the road and the coveted symbol of eternal commitment.

"Look, Mom!" I burst into the door and threw my coat on the couch. "Look!" I held up my hand and fluttered my fingers. "Darius finally asked me to marry him. I thought he'd never ask."

"I'm happy for you," Mom said. "He's a good man. A little slow …" She smiled. "But good."

Three days later, my phone rang. "Can you come up to my place?" Darius asked. "I need to talk to you."

The hour drive flew by as my eyes caressed my ringed hand, resting on the steering wheel. The sun caught the diamond, sending millions of prisms dancing through the car. I struggled not to speed.

"What's up?" I flung myself into Darius' arms the moment he opened the apartment door. He gently put me away from him and walked to the window. I stood next to him, trying to see what had his attention.

"Well?"

He turned toward me. "I'm just not ready for marriage. I'm sorry."

"What?"

"I …" He raised his hands, palms up, and shrugged. "I'm just not ready."

"So, you're saying the engagement is off? Seriously?"

He took a step back. "I'm sorry."

"Four years of waiting and all you can say is *sorry*?" I took a step forward. "You expect to string me on forever? Not a chance." I yanked the ring from my finger and tossed it to the floor.

"I love you, but I can't take this on-and-off relationship any longer. Don't call me. Don't call my family. I don't ever want to see you again." I spun on my heel and headed for the door. "I'm done."

I moved again. This time to Idaho.

❧ ❧ ❧

"You'll never guess who called," Mom told me a few months later.

"Who?"

"Darius."

"Darius? What did *he* want?"

"Says he became a Christian and wants us to go to his baptism."

"So, will you?"

"Of course not, Katie. Not after the way he treated you."

"Thanks, Mom. I appreciate that."

He'll be all alone, I thought later. *His family doesn't care, and besides, they live — what did he tell me? — some 14 hours away.*

A few days later, my phone rang.

"This is Darius."

"So? What do you want?"

"I wanted to tell you that I'm a Christian now."

"Of course you are." Surprise and then amusement invaded my tone. "You just want to worm your way back into my life," I scoffed.

"No, no. I'm being real here. Katie, God changed my heart."

"Yeah, right. Just because I became a Christian during our *non*-relationship, you think you can jerk me around again."

"No, Katie. I'm serious here. I love God, and I love you. I've found a real relationship with him, and I want a relationship with you, too."

We renewed our friendship, mostly by phone because of the distance between us. My job required a lot of traveling.

"I'm going to be in town next Friday night," I told Darius over the phone.

"That's great. I'm coaching a game for our church youth that night. Will you come?"

"Sure."

I met him at the gym. After the game, he drew me to one side. "Katie, we need to get married."

I felt my hands stiffen. "Really?"

"Yes, I love you. I want us to be together — forever. I'm ready to get married now. Let's get married right away."

"What about my job? I couldn't leave until next February."

"I can't quit my position, either," he said.

"What's the point of getting married and then living separate?" I asked.

"I just want to prove to you that I'm ready to commit to you. It's temporary," he said, meaning the geographical separation. "We can make it work."

After a two-month engagement, we married, honeymooned and then returned to our respective homes

— five hours apart. We lived single during the week and married on the weekends. Darius attended my church with me, and I saw firsthand the changes in him.

"I can't do this any longer," I said, five months into our part-time marriage. "I'm going to resign and move in with you."

"Baby, that's the best news ever. Welcome home!"

ॐ ॐ ॐ

"I'm pregnant," I announced a month after finally moving in with my husband.

"Baby, that's fantastic!" Darius wrapped me in a huge bear hug. "I can't wait to be a daddy. It's going to be great."

I can wait. I've never been big on babies. Dad raised a tomboy. I never much liked dolls and all that maternal, girly stuff.

"Now that we're going to have a family, we need to buy a house and get out of this apartment."

"A real house would be nice," I agreed.

The day came for signing the ownership papers of our new home. Just as we headed for the door, cramps seized my body, and I clutched at my three-months-pregnant belly.

"I'm having cramps." Panic crept into my voice.

"You'll be fine," Darius said. "Hurry up, we can't be late." He dashed down the steep concrete steps outside our apartment.

We drove to our realtor's office, signed the necessary documents and returned home. Darius took the steps two at a time and turned at the top landing.

"Come on," he urged.

I stared up at him, tears blinding me. "I need help. The cramping is worse."

"You're fine," he said.

I pulled myself up the stairs and headed to the bathroom. Horrified, I stared at the blood in the toilet.

"I think I'm losing the baby," I said, sobbing.

"Oh." He poked his head in the door. "I guess we should go to the hospital, then."

Life moved in slow-mo and fast forward all at the same time. *I can't believe this is happening,* I thought as the nurse wheeled me into a room. Darius stood in silence, gazing out the window.

Later, the attending doctor walked into my room. "Here is your baby," he said, handing me a tiny container. I clutched it to my chest as tears ran down my face. Darius turned and shook the doctor's hand.

"Thank you for your help, doctor."

"I'll give you two some time alone." He left, and Darius turned back to the window again.

"Darius," I cried. "I can't take this." *Come over here and hold me,* my heart begged while my lips remained mute.

"We'll have more kids," he said. "Everything will be fine."

My empty arms and belly ached, but I quickly learned to save my tears for when Darius was out of the house. The lack of emoting that attracted me before now crushed my soul.

"I'm pregnant," I told Darius in November, five months after the miscarriage.

"See, I told you everything would be fine."

I turned away. Disappointment morphed to anger. *Would it kill you to show just a smidgen of excitement?*

This time, I embraced the pregnancy and counted the days until I held our precious bundle in my arms.

"Open this gift." I thrust a wrapped shirt box into my mom's hands on Christmas Day.

"Okay." She busied her hands with the wrapping with a quizzical look at my grinning face. Then she lifted the lid, uncovering booties, a binky and a tiny bottle.

"We're pregnant!"

"Honey, I'm so happy for you both." Mom leaped up to hug us. Dad smiled from his chair.

৵৵৵

The moment Darius held his newborn son Joshua in his arms, he checked in as full-time dad but checked out as husband.

"We need to learn to communicate," I told him for the hundredth — or was it the thousandth? — time.

"About what?" He turned a blank face toward me before turning back and cooing over Josh.

"We never talk."

"About what?" he repeated.

"You know — *talk*."

"What do you want me to say?"

"I don't know. Ask me about my day. Ask me how I feel."

"Okay, how was your day?" Darius tickled Josh's tummy. Josh squealed.

"Oh, you just don't get it." I stomped into the kitchen and started throwing pans on the stove. *Men are so obtuse.*

Our pastor announced a marriage retreat three months after Josh's birth.

"We need to go," I said.

"If you think so." Darius shrugged. "Sign us up."

We gained one thing, and one thing only, from the retreat. Another pregnancy.

"Daddy's home!" Darius announced every day, flinging the front door open. He swept 15-month-old Joshua in his arms and carried him to the crib where newborn Marcus slept. "That's your brother," he said, tipping Josh so he could gaze on the youngest family member. "We're going to have so much fun together."

"How was your day?" I asked, wiping my hands on a kitchen towel and leaning in for a kiss.

"Fine." His lips briefly touched mine. "Let's go for an airplane ride!" He swung Josh high in the air and then dropped him between his legs. Up and down. Up and down. Josh's delighted squeals pierced through me.

I slammed through meal preparations.

"Dinner's ready."

Darius trotted into the kitchen with Josh on his shoulders. He lifted him down and settled him in his highchair. "You going to be a big boy and eat everything on your plate?"

Josh picked up his spoon and banged it against his tray. My head throbbed.

"Bow your head so Daddy can pray for the food."

I dropped the platter of chicken next to Darius' plate with a thud. "Look, Josh, chicken. Your favorite."

I slapped the mashed potatoes down next. "And mashed potatoes. Yum-yum."

I felt invisible.

≈≈≈≈

"I really want to coach," Darius said when Marcus was 8 months old. "I love kids, I love coaching. The university offers a program where I can get my master's degree in 13 months. I want to do this."

"Whatever."

"The school also offered me a job as assistant coach. It'll help pay my tuition."

I scowled and shrugged.

"Go follow your dream, buster," I snarled under my breath as I picked up the endless toys scattered all over the living room floor. "Leave me at home all day and all night, with two kids while you get to do exactly what you want to do and when you want to do it."

Darius worked toward his degree, while I concentrated on irreconcilable differences.

"I got a great job offer in Vancouver, Washington," Darius said after he held the coveted degree in his hand.

"I don't want to move."

"This is a great opportunity," he said.

"For you. I hate big cities. You know that."

"What about our boys? A city has far more to offer them, too, than this tiny town."

"I don't want to go," I repeated, my voice rising with each word.

"You would deprive me of this super position?" Ever-calm Darius only blinked.

"You're going to do whatever you want, anyway." I slapped Marcus' empty bottle on the kitchen table. "You always do."

We moved to Vancouver, and I dragged my growing resentment with me. We found a church to attend as a family unit, then scattered our separate ways when we returned home — Darius with his two sons, and me, looking on, outside their bubble of contentment. We drifted further and further apart.

"You're never home," I complained while scattering cheerios on Marcus' highchair tray. "You leave the house earlier and earlier."

"I don't want to start my day with hassling."

"You come and go as you please, while I'm stuck here, 24/7, with two toddlers."

Darius pushed his chair back, took his dirty plate to the sink and left the kitchen.

"I can't do this any longer." I marched out after him. "I'm going home."

"Fine. If you want to go, then go."

I collected our two sons and moved in with my parents. After cooling off for a month, I reconsidered my decision.

Thanksgiving and Christmas are coming. Do I really want to deprive Josh and Marcus of their daddy for the holidays?

I returned to Vancouver to try again.

જ✦જ✦જ

"I'll be right back," I told my boys the following February. "Mommy's going out to warm up the car."

I dashed outside and turned the motor on. Then I ran back into the house and hurried them into their jackets before herding them to the door.

"What?" Marcus bumped into my shins as I suddenly stopped at the front door. "Where's the car?"

I dialed Darius' number with trembling fingers.

"Somebody stole … stole … stole the … the car!" I choked through hysterical sobs.

"Did you call the police?" The measured tone I adored in college now drove me nuts.

"Of course I did."

"We'll talk about it when I get home. I have to get back to work now."

"How can you be so calm?" My voice raised an octave and ended with a ceiling-high squeak.

"I'm sorry about the car." Darius' tone remained calm.

"Sorry! That's all you can say? Obviously someone's been *watching* me. I left the car alone less than five minutes."

"But, you're okay."

"Okay? I'm freaking out here, and all you can say is I'm okay?"

I pounced on Darius the moment he got home.

"Someone has been casing the house," I shrieked. "What are you going to do about it?"

"I'm going over to Tim's to watch a sports special."

"You're *what*?"

"Katie, what good is flipping out? The car is stolen. The cops will find it. You're okay. The boys are okay. I'm going to Tim's now. Bye."

Our marriage frosted over like the Sandy Glacier in the Cascades. I refused to speak to Darius, and he refused to engage in verbal sparring.

"I'm totally done with this," I told my mom over the phone. "Even though the cops retrieved our car, Darius acts like the whole incident was nothing more serious than a spilled cup of coffee. He doesn't care about me at all. I'm coming home. This time it's final."

I called him at work a few days later. "I just want you to know that my dad is here. He has a U-Haul, and I'm moving home for good."

"You're not taking my kids away from me!" Darius yelled.

"Oh, yeah, I am."

Whoa! I finally found a way to extract some emotion from Mr. Cool-as-a-cucumber.

"We're leaving now."

"You stay put. I'm coming right now." The line went dead.

Crud.

I tossed a few Pull-Ups in a bag and hustled the boys to the car for the five-hour drive.

Gotta get out of here before he gets home.

My phone rang the next day.

"I drove straight to an attorney's office after I saw you'd skipped out on me."

I reveled in hearing anger in his voice. *At last! There's some emotion in the man after all.*

"So?"

"I filed for divorce."

"You *what?*"

"You heard me right." His tone hardened. "I filed for

divorce *and* visitation rights. Nobody's taking my sons from me."

"I just ..."

"Go on and tell your mom everything. You always do. You'll have plenty of time to bash me now that you're living with them. You're always nagging at me to communicate. Well, here's a news flash for you. You haven't even begun to see how ugly I can get. I will fight 'til my last breath for my kids."

Oh, God. I hoped for emotion, but I didn't expect it to come to this. Fear laid an icy hand on me, but I shook it off. *Let him fight. I'm ready.* My eyes narrowed as I clicked the *end call* button.

తతత

I got a job and found a place to rent in my hometown. Every other weekend, Darius and I met at a halfway point to transfer our sons and repeated the trip two days later. We'd kiss our sons hello or goodbye, depending on which leg of the trip we were on. Not one word passed between us. We communicated strictly through the lawyers.

Summer came, and Darius got the boys for a three-week stretch. I returned to my empty house and crawled into my cold bed. *Darius and I are both Christians. We faithfully attend church. How has it come to this? How?*

I'd become a Christian in college. I started going to church with a college friend. Then Mom gave me a book about the last days on earth. With images of the 9/11 devastation flashing across the news every day, I truly wondered if the end of the world was upon us.

After one service at my friend's church, I made a commitment to follow Jesus.

"I'm afraid to die," I told the pastor. "So many bad things are happening in the world that I could be killed at any time. I want to know my future is secure in God."

"Do you believe that Jesus came to earth to save us from our sins?"

"Yes, I do."

"Well, then, according to John 3:16, because you believe, you will 'not perish but have eternal life.' Do you want to pray now and accept Jesus into your heart?"

After that, I found a radio station that offered a lot of teaching and listened to it at every opportunity. I had also told Darius that all pre-marital sex would stop.

Then Darius became a believer and showed that Jesus was real in his life. That is, real toward his sons, his fellow teachers and his students. Somehow, he and I had slipped into married strangers.

I lay in bed, alone with my thoughts. *How could we drift so far apart as to be seeking divorce?* No answers came to my harried brain. Anxious thoughts paralyzed me. I lay all that day and night and well into the next.

"I can't take this anymore." My sobs echoed in the empty room. "I'll find my gun and kill myself. Then Darius will get what he wants — the boys — and I'll get what I need — peace."

I stumbled to the garage and searched for our rifle. "Where is it?" I cried out loud, after rummaging in every corner. "Oh, no! I think Dad took it home when I moved up here. What will I do now? I can't face another day."

I crawled back into bed. My body shook with deep, despairing sobs. Another full day passed. The following morning I sensed something I'd never felt before. I felt like God said, *Get out of that bed, and lay down before me.*

I obeyed. I stretched out, face down, on the floor beside my bed. I prayed. I wept. I waited. *Nothing happened.*

"Where are you, God?" I cried. "I'm doing exactly what you told me to do, and yet you feel a million miles away. Why are you treating me like this?"

Get up and out of this house, I sensed God say next.

I struggled to my feet, slipped into my sneakers and shuffled out the door. I began walking along the dirt road, my spirits as low as the soil under my feet. But as I walked, I felt lighter — and lighter.

What's going on here? I began humming and then singing. *Amazing grace, how sweet the sound.* The farther I walked and the longer I sang, the lighter I felt. Suddenly, a sensation of God's love washed over me. I knew in a new way that he'd never left me and had always been by my side through every battle, disappointment and loss.

"I'll get help, God. I promise. I know you don't want me to live this way anymore."

I pushed myself to go to church the following Sunday. Our pastor spoke on having a relationship with God.

"It's not about feelings," he said. "Feelings come and go. One day you can feel on top of the world and the next day in a ditch. Feelings are fickle and fleeting.

"You have to learn to stand on the promises of God. Many times in the Bible, God promised his people that he would 'never leave or forsake them.' Do you believe that? Even in the tough times, times of confusion and despair, do you believe that God is with you? Or do you have to *feel* his presence. Are you going to rely on your *feelings* or on what *God says*?"

I mulled over his words as I prepared my lunch. "God, I'm sorry," I prayed, sitting alone at my table. "I have been complaining to you all these years about Darius and his lack of emotion and his insensitivity to my needs and him ignoring my many demands. I'm sorry for putting a burden on him that only you can handle. He cannot be my everything. Only *you* can. From now on, I am going to pray for Darius as though he is simply my brother in Jesus and not as a failing husband."

"How are you doing?" I asked Darius at another of our son exchanges.

"What do you care?"

"I do care. I'm praying for you."

"Yeah, right. Praying for me to become the Mr. Perfect you're always nagging about."

"No. I'm sorry about that. I'm seeing a counselor now, and he's showing me what *I* need to change in *my* life."

"Sure you are."

He slammed his car door shut and drove off without a backward glance.

"Hey, kiddos. How was your time with Daddy?"

"Fun!" The boys bounced into my open car.

"We will pray for Daddy together, okay?"

๛ ๛ ๛

As the months passed, Darius' anger faded, and he began listening to me. He began counseling with the same therapist I was seeing, and they conducted their sessions over the phone.

"You know, you reminded me of my mother," Darius said, "when you tried to control my life through nagging."

"Why?"

"Mom controlled every aspect of our lives. She laid out my clothes until I was in the eighth grade. Appearances meant everything to her, and she kept everyone on a tight leash to make sure we didn't sully the image she built of a perfect family."

"And I transferred all the anger I held against my father onto you," I said. "I'm sorry for that. You are nothing like my dad, and you didn't deserve my spite."

Darius still hadn't stopped the divorce proceedings, so I had to drive back to Vancouver for the hearing.

We sat together in the foyer, talking, much like our first years together — only better now with the new open communication. His lawyer walked up just as we shared a laugh.

"Hey, we can't have this," he said. "We've got to appear before the judge in a few minutes for your final decree of divorce."

"Oh, yeah. Sorry."

We followed him into the courtroom. I sat on one side and Darius on the other.

"You are citing irreconcilable differences?" The judge addressed Darius. "Is this correct?"

Darius looked at him.

"Sir, you asked for this divorce. Do you want it or not?"

Darius looked over at me and then back at the judge. He remained silent.

"What are you going to do? Do you want the divorce or not?"

Darius looked at me again and back at the judge.

"Well, I guess I do."

"You guess? You can't guess. You either want the divorce or you don't."

"Uh, sure."

"Fine." His gavel cracked the silence with a resounding thud. "Divorce granted."

We signed the legal documents and walked out of the courthouse together.

"I guess it's real." Darius looked a bit dazed.

"Yes, we're really divorced now."

We stood on the steps in an awkward silence.

"You have a long drive home. You want to go for dinner?"

"Sure. Thanks," I said.

"It's a date, then."

"Guess it is." I laughed.

Instead of switching the kids at the halfway point of Iceberg Lane and Frigid Road, Darius began making the five-hour drive to visit them and *me*. We started applying the principles our counselor taught us to build a solid relationship.

"I have something important to tell you all," Darius told us the following July. "I feel God wants me to move here to be closer to you."

"Here?" Josh yelled.

"Here?" Marcus echoed, bouncing like a rubber ball all over the living room.

Darius grinned but sighed to me. "It means a huge cut in opportunity and pay, you know. But …" He looked at our sons, jumping and celebrating. "It'll be worth it."

"It sure will."

"We're going to pray that Daddy moves next door," Josh said. Marcus grinned.

Darius got a good job at a nearby university and found a house — not next door — but only a block from us. The boys were ecstatic. After his move, we began attending counseling sessions together.

"I want you to go through the book *Love & Respect*," our counselor suggested.

"What is that?"

"It's built on Ephesians 5:33. 'Each one of you also must love his wife as he loves himself, and the wife must respect her husband.' In most marital conflicts, the husband feels disrespected and the wife, unloved. This book will teach you how to overcome these issues and show you how to communicate effectively."

ॐ ॐ ॐ

Darius walked over to share Christmas morning with us. We sat on the couch together as the boys ripped open their presents.

"I'll make us some breakfast," I said, wading through mountains of brightly colored wrapping paper.

"Mommy, Mommy, come back," Josh called.

"What's up?"

"You left one present under the tree."

"I don't think so," I said. "I'm sure we opened them all."

"One more, one more," Marcus chirped.

Darius leaned over and pulled a tiny box from the branches.

"The boys are right," he said, grinning at me. Josh took the box and thrust it in my hands.

"Open it! Open it!" they chanted.

A beautiful diamond ring winked up at me.

"I'm ready to try again, Katie." He got down on one knee. "Will you marry me — again?"

"Are you serious?" I looked down at him and then at our two boys, bursting with excitement.

"Say yes! Say yes!"

"Of course I will." I threw myself in Darius' strong arms, and the boys threw theirs around both of us.

"Daddy's coming home!" Josh shouted. "Mommy said yes."

"I can't believe you're going through with it," Mom said to me one day while we shopped in Walmart. "After all he's done to you."

"Mom, I am just as responsible for the breakdown in our marriage. And now, Darius and I are learning how to build a healthy relationship. We will succeed this time because we are making God's principles the basis of our marriage."

And I'm learning to work out our issues privately and not come running to you anymore. I have too much respect for my husband to do that any longer.

"This sounds crazy, Mom, but divorce is the best thing that happened to both of us."

"You're right. It does sound crazy. How could divorce possibly be a good thing?"

"Because Darius and I tried to fix our marriage within our own abilities. Only when we gave up and turned it all over to God could it work out. We both had to learn to rely on God's strength and wisdom and stop relying on our own."

"I accept that," Mom said. "Have you chosen a date to marry?"

"Yes. Valentine's Day."

"I'm sure the boys are happy about all this."

"They are beside themselves."

☙☙☙

Since our remarriage, Darius and I have had a chance to share our story with other couples at our church, encouraging them to find hope, even when their marriage is falling apart at the seams.

"We are humbly grateful to tell you that God is able to heal marriage." Darius addressed the audience at one such seminar. "But he can't do it until you quit focusing on your spouse's failings and shortcomings."

"No spouse can be your everything," I added. "Only God has the power to be *everything* you need."

"You have to stop trying to fix the marriage on your own, and start asking God to do the impossible."

"And, trust me …" I paused and smiled at Darius. "He'll start on your own heart before he works on your spouse's!"

"Let go of your pride." Darius grinned back. "Believe me, when you let go and let God, *he* works it out better than you or I ever could. Katie and I are living proof of what God — and only God — can do."

BEYOND RESCUE
THE STORY OF RILEY
WRITTEN BY ANGELA WELCH PRUSIA

"You're going down." I pounded another nail into my weapon and targeted my buddy David. Everyone in our small town gossiped about his mother's mental problems, but that didn't stop our friendship or our friendly games of war.

David flashed a toothy grin and attached a rubber band to the metal head on his rubber band gun. "Take cover. Or die."

I rounded the corner in our basement and heard my father bellow from the top of the stairs. "Riley? Where are you, boy?"

I froze mid-stride. His heavy footfall meant he'd had a bad day working at the rail yard. And bad days equaled a thrashing for me.

If only I could hide.

But the basement shelves left no room to contort my growing 10-year-old body behind them.

"What're you doing?" My father filled the doorway with his menacing presence. Red flooded his face.

David's eyes widened. He'd never seen this side of his scoutmaster.

"Having a rubber band war," I stammered.

My dad ripped the board from my hand and swung. I

braced myself for the blows, but the impact made me cry out.

Metal shredded my flesh. Blood spurted and blurred my vision. I swiped at my face. The look in David's eyes stung worse than the beating. My body eventually numbed to the blows. But his horror stirred the shame I'd stuffed for years.

"You say my mom's crazy?" David screamed at my dad. "But you're nuts!" He tore out of the basement like a mad man.

My father stopped long enough to blame me for having a witness.

"You're a pathetic excuse for a son." He cursed. "You'll never amount to anything."

The words stung, but I closed my eyes and waited until his anger finally subsided.

☙☙☙☙

Like me, my sister Rachel endured the worst treatment from our father.

Our older brother Steven could do no wrong. My father wouldn't hurt the golden boy. People in town were always complimenting my father on Steven's perfect grades and achievements with Boy Scouts. He even appeared on a local television show in our area and earned a spot in the governor's band. My father ate up the attention.

No place in our home was safe for my sister. If Rachel

locked the bathroom door while she bathed, our father would kick the door open. When I stuck up for her, I paid the price. Rachel wouldn't tell me specifically what she'd suffered with him, but sometimes she would cry on my shoulder.

Mom tried to protect us, but she provided little comfort. She had her own daily battle to survive. Dysfunction ruled our home.

The one time Mom threatened to leave filled me with unspeakable terror. *How would we survive life if left alone with Dad?* But Mom came out of her hiding place, resolved to stick with her family.

No matter the cost.

The sound of Dad pummeling Mom's flesh behind closed doors made my stomach turn.

I wanted to save her, but my own body was often so raw, I couldn't move. The worst was when Mom stepped between me and Dad to deflect his blows. Every punch she endured was a knife to my heart.

કે કે કે

I hated going to school with the brutal evidence displayed all over my body, but we lived in a time and day when people looked the other way. No one reported the abuse. With my bad grades, I'm sure some people figured I deserved a good whipping.

My dad was a respected scoutmaster and a former Marine. The pastor where my mom attended church had his suspicions, but he never reported my dad to the authorities. The few times an adult told my dad to lay off, I paid dearly.

ھھھ

"Take that." I grabbed my brother's shirt one afternoon. His favored status as Dad's golden boy made him a target for my anger.

"Let go of me!" Steven yelled. But I was strong. And Dad's boxing lessons served me well.

I threw him against the closet wall, and a door popped open. Bottles of liquor shone in the muted light. I ran my hand along a case and muttered a curse word.

Steven used my distraction to escape.

Dad drank less than a six-pack a year, but he fueled his popularity by giving alcohol to friends.

I licked my lips, staring at the cases of alcohol. Mom had given me enough dinnertime sips of her white wine to know that the power intoxicated me.

Desire rippled my skin. I craved the tingly way the amber liquid coated my insides, dulling the pain.

Alcohol became my comfort and salvation before my 11th birthday.

ھھھ

Teachers thought I spent too much time daydreaming, but I retreated to the fantasy world inside my head when alcohol couldn't bring relief. Most days after school, I stole a bottle from Dad's stash and hurried to do my chores. Better to avoid being inside the house when Dad returned from work.

One afternoon, the neighbor boys and I played on a pile of dirt behind our house.

"Why don't we bury each other?" someone suggested.

The damp soil felt cool to my skin as my friend Sam and the others packed dirt around my torso.

"Cover his arms." Sam pointed to my bare flesh peeking through the dirt.

A shadow fell over me. Steven stared at me with a sinister look.

"Not so tough now, huh?" He covered my head with an old water bucket.

"Quit playing." My words rang in my ears.

Panic seized me. I couldn't breathe.

Steven didn't care. He was out for blood.

I felt myself losing consciousness when Dad grabbed the bucket. Strong arms freed me from the dirt. Later, one of the neighbor girls told me she saw what happened and ran for help.

It was the only time I know of that my dad ever spanked my brother.

A few years later, I heard my sister scream for help. When I found her in the closest, my brother was yanking off her clothes.

I gave Steven a beating he'd never forget.

᭘᭘᭘

By high school, I consumed large amounts of hard alcohol to dull the emotional toll of my father's abuse. When I saw my friends with their fathers, "why" questions taunted me. *Why did my father arouse fear and hate? Why didn't he love me? What did I do to provoke his hatred?*

Report card time made me break out in a cold sweat. No matter what I did, I couldn't earn the grades Steven did. My freshmen year, I stared at the D- knowing I couldn't hide the grade. Better to brace for the worst than prolong the inevitable.

I handed the report card to my dad without a word. But this time when the red flooded his face, I snapped and punched him in the face.

His surprise heightened his rage. I was no match for the former boxer. Dad pounded me with a vengeance, while Mom screamed for us to stop and my sister yelled for me to hit him again.

Hours later, when bruises dotted my face, Dad gave me a rare compliment. "I respect you for sticking up for yourself." He eyed Steven, who sat across the room watching the entire episode. "Unlike your brother."

The words hit their intended mark, and I saw defeat wash over my brother's eyes. Steven did everything to please my father. I felt no pride, only hurt for my brother.

I couldn't hide the black and blue bruises covering my face and body the next day at school. But I'd gotten so accustomed to the abuse, I excused him by saying I deserved the beating. If only I could do better at school.

If only I was a better son.

❧❧❧

Drugs became another weapon in my arsenal to combat the pain.

"You want to try some?" A friend handed me some marijuana one day while we hung out.

My eyes widened. "Where'd you get it?"

"From the truckers."

He worked at a truck stop, so he had easy access to drugs. Soon I experimented with hash, speed and LSD. My aversion to needles was the only reason I kept away from heroin. Hallucinations got me in some dangerous situations. Marijuana became my drug of choice.

After graduation, I found work on an oil rig, which provided a steady income for my drug use. I continued to numb my childhood pain and loneliness, seeing no reason to stop. Plus, there were other perks to my habit. I fell in with a group of girls who were more than willing to provide sexual favors in return for drugs.

What I longed for was a real friend.

I had none.

Drugs were my true friends.

❧❧❧

After a two-year stint working at a packaging company in another state, I returned home to work at a salt plant. I started as a laborer and worked my way up to management.

The other two secretaries hated the one called Nancy, a red-haired beauty and a tease. Encouraged by their pettiness, I lifted her long ponytail. "Looks like the same view as the backside of a horse."

Nancy fled the room in tears.

My heart broke. I stormed out of the room, wondering when I'd turned so cold. I was a pathetic excuse for a human being.

The next day I made a public apology to Nancy, and we quickly became good friends. We hung out regularly, and she'd even go hunting with me.

Nancy told me she asked her church to pray for me, but I wanted nothing to do with her Christianity. Every Saturday and Tuesday night, she invited me to attend church with her the following day. I feared God enough to believe I was headed to hell. But I couldn't accept her invitation. Not when I saw Christians as weak hypocrites. My mom had forced me to attend church as a kid, but no one there protected me and my sister. I hated Christians.

❦❦❦

I used to panic when my marijuana stash got below an ounce, but soon my old friends, drugs and alcohol, began to disappoint me. Instead of dulling my pain, they heightened my depression.

My bubble began to break. Memories began to assault me. Flashbacks turned to nightmares when I lay my head on my pillow.

"I feel like my 'best friends' are turning on me," I confided to another user. But she just stared back with empty eyes.

The pain was too much. Depression enveloped me in black. I wanted to end my life.

Attempt #1 failed. I couldn't even remember the details when I came to consciousness.

My overdose with Attempt # 2 terrified me. Moments before blacking out, I saw a vision of something so terrifying, I concluded it must be hell. I felt powerless to change my destiny.

Four days later, I woke up. A killer headache plagued me for weeks, reminding me of my pitiful existence.

A month passed, and the darkness got thicker. I couldn't take it anymore, so I decided to try suicide one more time.

"How did you live through everything you endured?" Steven had asked me during a rare candid conversation. The brother who never partied as a teenager fell hard for drugs and alcohol after high school. He couldn't keep friends or wives with his arrogant attitude and his crude sexual remarks.

My hands trembled. I couldn't stuff the childhood fears and terrors any longer.

"These might help." He'd handed me a handful of his prescription pills. "They speed up your heart. Take too many and you'll die."

His warning only fueled my hunger. I emptied the pills into my hand, ready to welcome death.

A knock interrupted my attempt.

"What do you want?" I barked.

The woman, a fellow user, wanted to do drugs.

"I'm fed up with everything. Drugs aren't helping," I confessed. "My brother gave me some pills."

"Well, I don't think you should do that." She turned and left without another word.

"Really?!" I wanted to scream.

I fell back against my couch, dumbfounded. I practically told the woman I was going to commit suicide, and her pitiful response angered me. I longed for a real friend. Her lack of feeling flooded me with anger.

I clenched the pills, ready to end it all. Darkness closed around me. I mentally paged through every relationship in my life. No one would really care if I was gone. My life had no value.

Another knock interrupted my black thoughts. I wanted to smash down the door.

But Nancy stood there like she did every Tuesday night. "Want to come to church with me tomorrow?"

Her question hit a nerve. Drugs. Alcohol. Women. Suicide. I'd done everything I could to end the pain. And nothing worked. *Why not try God?*

๛๛๛

I'd never considered God until that moment. But somehow, God read my heart and immediately began to change me. My desire for alcohol and drugs left the second my heart shifted. I stopped swearing and quit talking dirty.

Hunger to know God consumed me. A few months after attending church regularly, I felt God's presence overtake me. When the pastor asked if anyone wanted to surrender to Jesus, I felt my Savior reach out his hand and take mine. He'd died in my place. Now my eternal father wanted to call me his child. *Come with me.*

I walked forward toward the altar to embrace my Savior.

God's word began to speak to me. I couldn't get enough of the Bible.

A few months later, I spent time alone in the Badlands. Surrounded by the desolate beauty of God's creation, I walked to a grove of cedar trees. God's presence once again enveloped me. Peace and joy engulfed my heart. I felt like I could explode with love. When I turned, I saw a vision of Jesus dressed in a tunic, holding a shepherd's staff. Compassion flooded his eyes.

I love you.

His words reached straight to my heart. I came undone.

My father on earth was temporary. There before me was the father I'd always longed to have. The father who sent his son who died on my behalf. The father who loved me despite everything about me that was bad.

In his presence, words failed me.

かかか

You need to do three things, I felt God tell me as I spent time in prayer and studying the Bible. *Forgive your dad for what he did to you. Forgive him for what he did to your mother. Ask your dad to forgive you for the bitterness in your heart.*

The first two were hard enough to swallow, but I trusted God and wanted to be obedient. The last request took some time to accept. My mom had died a few months earlier from a rare disease. In my heart, I felt the stress had taken its toll, and she'd finally given up. I needed to act quickly before my aging father also left this earth.

But, God, what did I do? I endured horrible treatment at the hands of the very person who should've loved me. Don't I have a right to be bitter?

Forgiveness isn't about your dad, I felt God say. *It's about becoming free. If you don't forgive, bitterness will bind you to him.*

I finally agreed. *How could I move forward in my life if I couldn't forgive my own father?*

I drove five hours to face my earthly father, and I couldn't do it.

When I returned home, I didn't feel condemned by God. Just prompted by him to try again, and the second time, I asked my dad for his forgiveness.

He couldn't have cared less.

But my obedience wasn't about my temporary father who lived on earth. Forgiveness was about the heart of God, my eternal father.

BEYOND RESCUE

❧❧❧

The more time I spent with God, the more I realized my identity. I didn't have to pass on the abuse I'd endured. I didn't have to turn into my father. Or my father's parents. God's blessing would change my future line.

Maybe I really could be the husband and father I never thought I could become.

Desire for a lifelong mate consumed my new prayer life. Every chance I had, I begged God for a wife.

One night a few months after the calendar year turned, I woke up from a sound sleep and sat up in bed in the hours before dawn.

You will not live alone, I heard a voice say in my head. *I have someone for you.*

A picture filled my mind of a woman I'd met while helping with the church Christmas play. Not long after that, I saw Carrie in the grocery store where she worked.

I wiped sweaty palms against my pants. "Will you go out with me?"

Her eyes narrowed, like I'd walked off a crazy bus. "Not in a million years."

Her response sent me reeling, so I went back to God in prayer. *Did I really hear from you?*

Some things God reveals aren't meant to be announced until the right time. Over the next several months, my attempts were met with resistance. I wanted to give up, but I believed Carrie was the one for me. I admired her long-held faith and wanted a wife who loved Jesus like she did.

How could I get her to see we were truly a match made in heaven?

Carrie finally agreed to help me study the Bible if we joined a group, but she refused to date me. When I complained to God, he would lead me to a passage in the Bible about having faith.

Learning patience wasn't easy, but I believed Carrie was worth the wait.

She eventually thawed, but not entirely. She shot down my marriage proposal. Still I kept pursuing her. And she invited me to meet her family. After attending her family reunion together, I couldn't wait any longer. I got down on one knee and asked Carrie to marry me.

"Not on your life," she replied.

My heart ached, but she consoled me by agreeing to pray about it.

A week later, I approached her. "Did you get an answer?"

Carrie nodded. "I have peace."

I resisted the urge to do a fist pump. I could accept God's peace.

When our son Mason arrived, I held him close to my heart, sure that if I wasn't careful, I would break his little frame. Tears slipped down my face. He was so small and trusting.

I was not only a husband, I was really a daddy.

BEYOND RESCUE

❧❧❧

I grew pretty close to a buddy of mine at the salt plant. He was a strong Christian man, and I began to look up to him, and he gave me advice as I continued to grow as a Christian. It was pretty ironic that God brought Max and me together that way, since he had once told our pastor that "even God can't save Riley."

But the book of Ezekiel tells us that God will remove our hearts of stone and give us a new spirit and a new heart. Before my encounter with Jesus, I was a mess, having done everything to dull my painful feelings by becoming cold and numb. But God filled my heart with love for him and love for people.

Now Max and I spent countless hours talking about the Bible. When I felt the desire to attend Bible college, Max encouraged me, so Carrie and I moved to Louisiana where I began pastoral studies.

Before I finished school, a children's home called with an opening for a house couple. Carrie embraced the opportunity. The idea scared me, but after our visit and interview, I understood what my wife meant by God's peace. It surpassed the anxiety I felt. God was with us.

I dropped my studies, and we packed our bags.

Working with kids who'd suffered abuse like I had brought heartache, but laughter brought relief. A co-worker said I wouldn't leave the same, and she was right. God changed my heart and gave me a passion for helping those in need.

After two and a half years, an opening at a youth ranch was an answer to prayer. With few breaks and little time off, I couldn't have continued at the children's home much longer before suffering a nervous breakdown.

I could identify with the toughest boys at the ranch, most of whom were on probation. I purchased model car kits for each one, and while we worked on them together at the end of the day, the boys often opened up to me. They were touched that I would buy them something with my own money. Some had questions when they saw me reading my Bible, and I loved sharing with them the hope I'd found.

Since Carrie and I were house parents again, our son Mason spent much of his childhood growing up alongside the boys we served.

On the tough days, God taught me to lean on him rather than on my emotions. That served me well since many of their stories mirrored mine.

I got my associate pastor's license and felt a tug on my heart for my old hometown.

I dug in my heels. The last place on earth I wanted to return to was the place that reminded me of my past. I begged God to send me somewhere else.

I asked friends and co-workers to join me in prayer.

God answered, but not the way I expected. He took us on a detour through Bend, Oregon, to bring me back home. Frustration and anger dimmed my faith, but Carrie's never wavered. When opportunities to pastor a church fell apart, we moved in with her parents.

"Why bring us to the Northwest only to shut the door?" I cried out to God one afternoon.

What is Bend? I felt God impress upon me.

"A place of turning."

Ask Carrie.

Hearing my wife's heart touched me; we moved back home.

The oil boom had died, and people needed help and encouragement. It was time to move home.

෴෴෴

For the next 17 years, God used Carrie and me as pastors to start a church and minister to people in my hometown. Sharing God's love was my passion. Serving the Lord by serving people brought me joy even on the hard days when people disappointed me.

Weight gain crept up on me after a painful knee injury left me sedentary. A series of health concerns began to plague me. With me bedridden and with no assistant pastor, our church membership dwindled.

"Say goodbye," the ambulance driver told Carrie before driving me off when gangrene poisoned my blood. "He's not going to make it to the hospital."

But God must have had other plans.

With the help of gastric surgery, I lost 250 pounds, and my health turned a corner. Unfortunately, medical bills wiped out our finances, so we made the hard decision to move closer to Carrie's family again.

Saying goodbye to our church family brought heartache, but we believed God wasn't done with us yet.

❧❧❧

Harvest Church quickly became home after our move to Oregon. Pastor Brad began encouraging me while I waited to see what God had planned for the next chapter of my life. I continued to trust God's word in 2 Timothy 1:12, which reads, "I know whom I have believed, and am convinced that he is able to guard what I have entrusted to him for that day."

If God wants me to pastor another church, my heavenly father will not disappoint.

❧❧❧

When I was a kid, I wanted to become a Marine in part to gain my father's approval, but a high school wrestling injury prevented me from joining. When my son joined the Marine Corps, I couldn't have been more proud.

Carrie and I said our bittersweet goodbyes the day Mason left for his overseas post. Every time he called or emailed, Mason couldn't share much. Carrie and I started many of our days on our knees begging God to protect our son. Despite the awful news reports from Iraq and Afghanistan, we had to trust God.

Now, almost a decade later, Mason is back home. He moved down the street and began work in the financial world. Maybe someday he will open up, but for now, his experiences remain locked inside. Surviving PTSD is a daily struggle for Mason.

"I'm thinking about getting a new job, Dad," he recently shared with me.

"Yeah?" I raised my eyebrows. I love the relationship we have, especially since I always longed for the same with my own father.

"The desk job just isn't the same as the Marines."

"I suppose not." I grinned. "What're you thinking?"

He didn't hesitate. "Working at a youth ranch."

A picture flashed through my mind of the little boy who played at the ranch in Montana where Carrie and I served as house parents. The same boy grew up to be the young soldier before me. War changes a man, and my son needs to find his own way back home.

Mason will come around. This temporary dad's praying to our eternal father. And his heart hears the cries of his children. After all, God even saved Riley.

UNSEEN ALLY
THE STORY OF PHILIP
WRITTEN BY DOUGLAS ABBOTT

I was 12 years old when Mom asked me to come into the living room with her. It was a bright, sunny day, but my mother's countenance was subdued. I'd never seen her with such a heaviness of sorrow in her eyes. Something was very wrong. By the time we settled into our seats, Mom was crying.

"Sweetheart," she started haltingly. "I did something awful when you were very little."

I waited, growing more apprehensive by the second. Her tears started flowing freely, blending with her mascara to create inky smears on her cheeks, which she kept wiping away.

"Mom —"

"No, let me finish. I hurt you, when you were only a baby. I was changing your diaper. Honey, I'm so sorry!"

"Sorry for what, Mom?"

"I touched you. Inappropriately. What I did was unforgivable." She broke off for a moment and sobbed into her hands. "I'm sorry for what I did. I don't know what made me do it. Please forgive me!"

I went to her and took her hand. "I forgive you, Mom. Of course. I love you."

It was all true. I did love her and forgave her. But her

disclosure profoundly disturbed me. I had no recollection of the incident.

However, it explained many things.

From my earliest memory, I'd felt like there was something wrong with me. It colored all my experiences — everything I did.

Who gets molested by his own mother? I wondered after talking with Mom that day.

It would take many years for me to get an answer.

ঞ‌ঞ‌ঞ

When I was 5, my family moved to Klamath Falls, Oregon. My upbringing was essentially stable. My siblings and I never lacked for any of our physical requirements.

However, we had our difficulties. Mom was bipolar. I discovered this by chance. One afternoon, when I was very little, I walked into the living room to find Mom frozen on the couch, crying.

"Mommy, what's wrong?" I asked.

Instead of answering, she just gazed at the floor. Tears spilled down her cheeks.

"Mommy!" I called, over and over. But she couldn't stop crying long enough to answer me.

I had believed both my parents were invincible. That day, the protective bubble (which I hadn't even known was there) punctured, and from then on, I felt the possibility of having to fend for myself at some point.

I also learned, as did my brothers and sisters, that

when Mom was depressed, we could get away with more of our shenanigans.

My father gave 100 percent for us. He may have tried twice as hard since he labored in the wake of his own father's irresponsibility. The man apparently fathered illegitimate children all over the country. That legacy — and the hardship Dad endured as a child — may well have marshaled Dad's resolve to live out his traditional values and provide for us in every way he could.

An ace mechanic, Dad worked at Caterpillar and created gadgets on the side when he wasn't at work. His strength and creative prowess inadvertently produced a contest among his children for his affection. My siblings and I all strove to outdo each other and win Dad's praise.

I seemed to be without any special talents and so contended constantly with feelings of inferiority. I often felt unaccepted and believed I had to perform well in order to be loved. My efforts to excel academically, athletically and artistically were overshadowed by my younger sister. Sarah was a child prodigy whose exploits made me look inadequate by comparison.

Because of my dyslexia, I experienced great frustration trying to read. I took no comfort in my ability to perform in other subjects. I sensed the importance of reading, and whatever wispy self-confidence I possessed shriveled because of my learning disability. I watched other children (including my own sisters) read without any difficulty, and I smoldered with envy. My burden grew worse when I was held back a grade and then had to attend classes with

Sarah. Each time we were asked whether we were twins, I had to endure the humiliation of explaining why we were in the same grade.

One afternoon, I sat in the school bleachers watching Sarah compete at a track meet. My father whooped every time she came into view or cleared a hurdle. I watched him smile with pride, the corners of his eyes crinkling with pleasure. I longed for him to feel the same way about me. However, I lived constantly with the idea that my father was unimpressed with me. In my mind, he took care of me because he was required to, not because he really loved me.

As I sat there, I heard low laughter above and to my right. I craned my neck and saw two boys from my third grade class looking down at me and smiling mirthlessly.

"He's a little retard. I heard he got held back a grade because he can't even read." More laughter followed.

I said nothing. The ridicule of my peers proved to me that love and acceptance must be earned by a good showing. My father had unwittingly taught me that lesson every time he lavished Sarah with praise but ignored me.

I never really felt honored by my father and grew up longing for a deep, unconditional love that I never received.

ॐ ॐ ॐ

When I was 8, I became interested in spiritual matters. My bedroom window looked out over a beautiful view, and I often gazed at it for long periods of time. One night after dusk, a fascination with angels became an overwhelming curiosity. As a slight breeze licked around the edges of the fields, trees and shrubs, I told God I wanted to see an angel. While I stood there, I felt certain I saw a human-like figure appear just for a moment in our yard. It was completely dark, but it seemed the creature glowed slightly. I could just make out the hem of his robe on the grass.

This was the first time I became aware of a transcendent world — something larger than human existence.

I discussed my experience with my father, who invited me to pray with him.

"Jesus died for you, son. He wants you to trust him with your life."

Sarah was there and prayed with us.

෧෧෧

A year later, I fell ill with pneumonia. I woke up with my lungs so full of fluid that I couldn't draw in a breath. I stumbled down the stairs and collapsed on the floor at the bottom, unconscious from lack of oxygen. While my parents scrambled, my body tried to discharge the fluid by vomiting while I went in and out of consciousness. It felt like trying to breathe through a clogged tube. Dad carried me into the bathroom, placed me next to the tub and ran hot water to generate steam, thinking the problem was phlegm in my airway.

"He's turning blue!" Mom screamed.

Next, as I continued fading in and out, Dad strapped me into the car to take me to the emergency room. I vaguely noticed how fast he was driving. The engine practically shrieked as we barreled through red lights. I heard the tires screeching as he turned the corners.

In and out. I saw doctors and nurses working urgently on me. I lay under a powerful white light. One of the nurses cut my clothes off, but I tried to pull them back over my body.

I woke up the next morning, clean and dry in a hospital bed. My lungs felt clear. Then I noticed the tubes coming out of my nose and mouth. I looked around and saw a respirator pushing oxygen into my body. It issued a strange hissing noise as its plunger went up and down like a little round accordion inside the tube.

"You're very lucky to be alive," my doctor told me.

It confirmed what I already suspected: *I had nearly died.* I felt the heaviness of the moment and sensed — for the first time but not the last — that my life would have a purpose.

&?&?&?

From time to time, Mom and Dad sprang for a sitter so they could have a date night. On one such occasion, they hired a couple we knew only marginally, the Andersons. Mom and Dad brought us to their house for the evening, apparently so the Andersons could go out themselves, leaving us in their house with their teenage kids.

After we had eaten dinner, the oldest boy, a 16 year old named Randy, brought me into his bedroom and told me to reveal my privates to him and the other kids. I don't know why I agreed. The experience brought a mixture of discomfort and a strange excitement. For years afterward, I felt guilty because of the secret pleasure it gave me.

I lived constantly with a sense of shame. I couldn't remember a time when I didn't feel like there was something wrong with me — something that separated me from everyone else. I believed the shame was part of me. The incident with Randy Anderson didn't teach me anything new — it affirmed what I already believed about myself due to my general ineptitude. The world sidelines those who have no standing. I had no reason to believe that the same principle didn't apply in families. It certainly seemed to in mine.

ॐॐॐ

Two years after we moved to Redding, California, I came home from school to find Mom losing her mind.

"Kids, go pack your suitcases. We're moving down to Riverside to stay with Aunt Sheila!" Mom was grinning ear to ear and making strange movements. She *looked* like Mom, but everything else was off. Furthermore, my father hadn't mentioned anything about this.

"Your dad's going to stay here," Mom said in response

to my questions. She remained smiling as though it was perfectly all right to cleave our family into pieces.

"C'mon, don't look so sad, Philip! We're going to go to Disneyland and do all sorts of fun stuff."

I was terrified. No one seemed prepared to challenge Mom's authority. I was convinced it was really going to happen. She was going to whisk us away from Dad, perhaps forever.

I ran out the front door and didn't stop running until I reached the extremity of our property, out behind a copse of oak trees. There, I found a shady spot, ensconced myself in the tall grass and started crying out to God. I was emotionally overwhelmed and hadn't the first clue what to even pray for. Nevertheless, my prayer tumbled out of my mouth. It was like no prayer I had ever prayed. The words weren't English but sounded like some faintly Slavic language.

I'd heard about prayer languages but had never tried to speak in one. However, I sensed that this was precisely what I was doing.

I prayed for a good while, letting strange vowels and consonants flow out of my mouth, remarking inwardly what a strange experience all this was. When I finished and rose to my feet, I felt a tremendous peace all through my being.

Back at the house, meanwhile, Dad had arrived home and calmed Mom somewhat. However, just an hour or so later, as tears coursed down my cheeks, I sat and watched through the living room window as my father drove Mom to the hospital. She wouldn't return for several days. Dad assured us that she would soon be coming home again, but I thought my whole world was coming apart.

భ్లిఫ్లిఫ్లి

During a visit with Mom at the hospital, I went to a small park on the grounds with Sarah and my brother Cliff. We found a pornographic magazine lying in the grass by an irrigation canal and immediately started thumbing through it. It had all the marks of an insignificant moment; the occasion was accompanied by laughter and juvenile remarks. However, the response of my body was incredibly powerful. My insides soared with a mixture of shame and exhilaration at the sight of those beautiful women fully displayed in their birthday suits. I felt my own desire crouch inside me like a wild animal.

Unlike Sarah and Cliff, I was deeply affected by the discovery of the magazine. The photographs introduced me to an underworld with different rules — a degraded place that matched the way I had long viewed myself. I didn't fit in with the world at large, but this one seemed like a custom fit.

భ్లిఫ్లిఫ్లి

I began to sense something completely new coming over me as my family settled into a new church in Redding. I kept hearing how real God is and how he speaks to everyone who is listening. The message came at a time when I was hungry for it.

My parents bought a trampoline and stationed it in the backyard. Oddly enough, I discovered that even more than the benefit of bouncing on it, I appreciated the trampoline because it provided a springy place to lie down in the evening.

I'd always loved looking up at the stars, and having the trampoline at my disposal made stargazing even more enjoyable. I took to sleeping outdoors. It was summer, and my developing habit was rarely disrupted by rainfall. The nights were warm — perfect for drifting off to sleep while I pondered creation. The stars made me think of God throwing a great handful of sequins against the bluish-black fabric of the sky. Only these sequins were each immense fireballs, many times the size of earth and so far away that they were reduced to tiny sparkles above me. The size and scope of it all overwhelmed me.

I began to sense God's presence, as though he was drawn by my growing admiration for his creative power. I started out sleeping alone under the stars. Before long, I felt I shared the experience with the stars' very creator.

One night, as I slept on the trampoline, I had a vivid dream in which the irrigation canal behind our house rose and bubbled up over its banks. The next morning, as my father drove us to church, I glanced over at the canal and saw that the water had risen several feet.

I asked my pastor about it.

"I can't tell you what it means, of course," he said

thoughtfully, stroking his chin. "It could be all kinds of things. You should pray about it. At the very least, it would seem God is inviting you into a more intimate prayer life with him."

I began to pray more focused prayers, asking God to speak to me through whatever medium he saw fit. That night, the weather forecast called for a rainstorm. As I stood on the trampoline, gazing up, I watched as clouds drifted in from the east and gathered over the moon. I could smell the rain in the air. I began to speak, telling God how beautiful and wondrous he'd made the world. As I prayed, I felt moved to ask for a sign. It seemed audacious at first, but the more I considered it, the more I was drawn to the idea.

"God, will you show me a sign that you are real?"

A moment after I asked, the air around me was suddenly charged with electricity. Every bit of exposed skin on my body tingled with it. I became enveloped by something I can only describe as liquid love. It was alive and moving and penetrated to the center of my being. I felt completely loved and accepted and had the undeniable sense of God there with me, expressing a love for me that could never change. The sense of shame and inadequacy left — melted in the force of God's presence. I knew then, beyond any doubt, that the shame was completely false. The truth was this: God loved me, and all I had to do was trust him.

I began to sense that there was more to come. I looked up and saw the clouds over the moon glowing with a rich luminescence. They stopped directly over the moon. Then, as I watched, a falling star emerged from the underside of the clouds and came directly toward me. Its tail sparkled behind it as it moved. The star grew larger and larger as it came toward me. Then, at its brightest point, it simply vanished from the middle of the sky. When it was gone, the entire mass of clouds it had emerged from lit up with a bright light.

Afterward, I stood motionless for a long time just looking up into the sky. At that moment, I became convinced that God was more real than the moon, the clouds, the trees or the trampoline under my feet. He was as real as if I had heard his voice and taken him in with my eyes.

I was amazed at how good I felt. I was completely at peace. For the first time in my life, I felt like a whole person, as deserving of life and of God's love as anyone else. I literally couldn't find the shame that had been with me from my earliest memory.

That was the last time I had any doubts about how real God is. That night and all the next day, I spoke about what I had seen with everyone who would listen. God had poured something bold and courageous into me. I had an unquenchable desire to tell everyone I met how wonderful Jesus is, how friendly and approachable.

ॐॐॐ

I finished secondary school and decided to pursue a ministry internship with a local church I attended. Because of my dramatic experience under the stars, I wanted to grow in my understanding of God, and he continued to become more and more real to me through successive experiences.

Over the next few years, I experienced God in many different ways. On one occasion, I was hit with an inexplicable joy and went into gales of uncontrollable laughter, tears rolling down my cheeks.

Another time, I had a vision while I was talking to God about a great big, shaggy dog who came bounding up to me, so excited to see me that his whole body shook in full-body wags. As I looked at the dog's face, I felt the presence of God again and sensed him telling me, *This is how much I look forward to spending time with you.* My father was a workaholic with little time to spare on his son when I was growing up. To receive a vision of God looking forward to spending time with me so very much, and in such a playful and joyful way, really finally showed me how much God truly loves me. It changed me forever.

These strange and enigmatic encounters brought up many questions and piqued my curiosity about God. What I learned about God and Jesus from church didn't seem to fit with the supernatural meetings I experienced. *Who was it that could overwhelm me with laughter and appear in the eyes of animals and so vividly in my daydreams?* As I sought answers to my questions, I learned more about God. That he is the father of all and creator of everything.

I learned more about Jesus. The same Jesus I had accepted so willingly so many years before, but had not truly known or understood until then. I learned that Jesus is God's one and only son. That he died to pay the price for every bad thing any person has ever done and, in doing so, provided the only way for any one of us to live eternally in heaven.

But my questions weren't completely answered until I finally discovered that, as the Bible teaches, God is a trinity — three persons which God comprises: the Father-Creator, the Son, Jesus, a third person as well, and the Holy Spirit, who works in the world today. He was the person of the trinity I encountered that starry night and so many times since then, I decided. From that day forward, the purpose of my soul was to not only introduce others to the goodness of God and to salvation through Jesus, but also to the power of the Spirit.

Through my personal experiences with the Spirit and deepening understanding of the Father and Son, I grew closer to God, and I felt myself getting to know him more and more. He faithfully and incrementally swept away the performance mandate under which I'd labored so unsuccessfully my entire life.

Little by little, I became convinced the Father was telling me, *I am not so concerned with your character or the sin in your life, but spending time with you.* Those encounters and my growing understanding of God, Jesus and the Holy Spirit worked a tremendous healing in me.

の の の

During my last year of high school, I got involved with an organization called Youth With a Mission, or YWAM, and began a series of short-term mission trips. All through that year, my desire to work in outreach solidified as I met many open-minded people all over America in malls and fairgrounds and coffee shops. I had an opportunity to return to Maui for a longer trip, but I sensed that God wanted me to stay in Redding. I felt like he was saying, *She is here.*

So I stayed in Redding and enrolled in community college. I also embarked on an internship with my church youth group. I continued to go on short-term mission trips.

❧❧❧

I began to notice a young woman around the church. I knew of Eva's involvement in mission trips. I liked her, though not in a romantic way. She was several years younger and still in high school. However, I learned that she had designs on me. So, at the urging of my friends, I spoke with her.

"Eva, I can't be with you."

"Why?"

"I can think of all kinds of reasons, but the main one is that I'm an intern here. I'm not allowed to be in a relationship as an intern. It's part of the deal."

She waited for me, all through my two-year internship, and even gave her consent when I told her I wanted to date other girls at the college. Her maturity astonished me. Even so, I remained clueless about where our relationship headed, despite the whole church whispering their guesses.

Toward the end of 1997, Eva and I spent an evening under the stars. As busy as we'd been, it was rare for us to be in the same place at the same time. We took advantage of it by adjourning ourselves to my favorite spot — the trampoline behind my boyhood home. It was a classic warm, starry night in Redding. We breathed in the floral fragrances and listened to the song of a mockingbird, a regular visitor to my mom's yard.

"How come you didn't write me more when you were in the Ivory Coast on your last mission trip?" Eva asked as we stretched out. Eva was only half serious. But, in fact, I *hadn't* written her much. The trip had been packed full of activities. Eva, on the other hand, had written me *every day* while she was on her own mission trip. To this day, I don't understand her devotion.

"Well, I don't know. I certainly should have." I smiled.

Eva gave me a playful punch in the shoulder. She grinned back. "Well, what are you going to do about it?"

I felt a great surge of inspiration just at that moment. "Well, you know, I was thinking: Married couples don't have to write as many letters to each other. So …"

Eva and I became engaged right there on the trampoline.

However, steps remained to be taken. I visited her father, Carl, who gave us his blessing — but not before

Eva's uncles asked to meet me after hearing of my engagement to their niece.

It was a drizzly morning when I arrived at my future father-in-law's home. Eva's uncles met us at the door and motioned toward the garage. All four of them were big, burly, bearded men who rode Harley Davidson motorcycles. Each of them carried a Bible in one hand and a rifle in the other. After we sat down, they asked me to tell them my testimony.

It began to feel like an interrogation. I felt unsure about whether my story would pass muster with these men, who obviously had very high standards for their niece. Eva had told me how previous suitors underwent the same scrutiny. One of them got thrown into a pond.

However, by the time I finished, most of them appeared visibly moved. They all hugged me, clapped me on the back and gave me their blessing.

We married in May 1998, flew to Maui for our honeymoon and stayed in a tree house in the rainforest.

ಌಌಌ

The following year, I graduated with a BA in missions. The year after that, I enrolled in the Bethel School of Supernatural Ministry. We went on periodic mission trips while I went through the curriculum.

Our lives were thrown out of kilter when Eva miscarried in 2000. We both had a profound desire for a family and were elated when Eva became pregnant. The pain was indescribable. For a time, we each struggled with fear — what if there were more miscarriages? Would we ever have little Philips and Evas to raise? We were almost afraid to try again after having our first child snatched away.

All through our pain and loss, however, we resolved to trust God for a family. We made a special trip to see our pastor, who prayed over us and blessed us. With every step and every prayer, we continually gave our grief and fear to God — and placed our desires for a family in his hands. After one very long childless year, our firstborn son, Jordan, came into the world.

❧ ❧ ❧

In 2002, as I approached the end of my curriculum at Bethel, Eva, Jordan and I moved to Mozambique, Africa, for an extended mission trip.

We returned to California in 2003 and welcomed Jacob into our family. Other than the happy introduction of a new son, it was a hard season. We had sold all our possessions and gone off to Africa with nothing but our suitcases. We were as dry as could be. However, Mom had us move in with her while we rebuilt. It was back to home base on the same property where I'd grown up. Everything was still there — the canal, the tree house and the trampoline in the backyard.

A kind soul loaned us a Prius and then gave it to us outright while I sought work. We weren't sure we wanted to be career missionaries. If we stayed in Redding, I would end up pursuing some other career. What kind of career, I could only guess at. Among our difficulties was our loss of energy and strength. Africa had been hard. All of us had been sick with malaria at different times. Eva contracted a parasite that took 30 pounds off her frame before she finally recovered.

Justin came along in 2006. I headed up a family of five and still wasn't clear about where we were going. God hadn't allowed us to so much as miss a meal, but our trust in him couldn't eliminate basic concerns. The dry spell was stretching on.

"Sweetheart, maybe we should go back to doing mission trips. We'll get by. This limbo is excruciating." Eva draped her arms over my shoulders.

"I know, honey." I nodded. "I hate it as much as you do. Do you really want to go back to the mission field? You know what we went through. You haven't even regained all the weight you lost in Mozambique."

Eva turned her palms up and laughed. "I'm fine. So is Jordan. We should do what God desires for us."

We continued praying. The fact was, neither of us felt God calling us back to the mission field.

Over the next year, the idea of teaching began to gather steam in my mind. I'd always felt a strong connection with children. Most of my work up to that time involved young people, from the internship in youth ministry to our mission trip in Mozambique, where there had been kids everywhere.

"I'm thinking about teaching, Eva." We were sitting at the kitchen table after a light lunch. "Maybe that's what I've been heading for all this time. What do you think?"

"I think it sounds marvelous. You have a way with young people. I've watched you." She gave me a dazzling smile.

I couldn't help smiling back. But I wasn't convinced yet. "Well, so do you. That doesn't mean I should be a teacher necessarily. But I have to say, I'm starting to get excited about the idea. Pray with me about it."

"Of course, honey."

So we did, and both of us got vibes that were almost electric. It was all the prodding I needed.

☞☞☞

We got chills when we visited Baker City. It was beautiful and picturesque.

We felt God inviting us to pitch our tent there. As with all the directives God has given me in my life, this was optional. I sensed the Lord saying, *If you move here, I will bless you.*

We traveled to Oregon with all our possessions in August 2007. It took two trips to get everything there. On the first trip, I asked God for a sign. "Lord, if this is your plan for us, bring rain to confirm your direction."

Sure enough, as we were in transit, we drove through a flat, arid place where we could see nothing but sand for miles all around. As we drove on, clouds gathered directly overhead and burst open with rainfall.

I started teaching at a school operated by a congregation called Harvest Church, a medium-sized fellowship that hung out the slogan "current without compromise." The school was called Harvest Christian Academy, the scholastic home of around 80 kids at the time. The academy has a slogan, too, which I took instantly to heart: "They shall be like a tree, planted by the rivers of water."

Teaching kids turned out to be a dream job. Children are endlessly honest, imaginative and pliable. I felt blessed to have the privilege of teaching them, praying with them, introducing them to the Holy Spirit and sharing my faith with them.

The city, the church and the job all felt handpicked for us. Without much deliberation, we soon found that we liked the church and its friendly congregants well enough to make it our church home.

I made fast friends with the children's pastor, Clay, who oversaw the Royal Rangers and the church's other youth ministries. In addition to my teaching responsibilities at the academy, I started helping with the Royal Rangers — a mentoring program that seeks to build Christ-like character and servant leadership into boys and young men in a relational environment, often in the context of recreational activities.

I was surprised when Clay asked me to be the guest speaker for a Royal Rangers campout. It was the biggest compliment I'd received in a long time.

The campout took place on a shared campground that

offered swimming, canoeing, hiking and many other activities. On the second night there, everyone gathered around a bonfire for worship music and sharing. There were two guitars and some songbooks. It was a gorgeous night.

When the time came for me to speak, I thought it best to simply describe the many times God had touched me — how often I had wondered at their age what people meant when they said, "God speaks to me."

"It isn't a formula," I said. At that point, most of the fidgeting and horsing around stopped. Many of these young people just listened to me, their honest eyes large with curiosity. "He wants to speak to you. All he wants is your attention. The Holy Spirit isn't scary. He is gentle and loving and brings wonderful peace with him wherever he is. He is an unseen ally who wants to make himself more deeply known to each of you."

I told them about an encounter another Royal Ranger had with the Holy Spirit.

At one of our Wednesday night Royal Rangers meetings, a sixth-grader named Chandler put his hand up when we asked if anyone wanted the opportunity to experience the Holy Spirit. I gestured for him to step up to me. "Everyone gather around Chandler here. We're going to pray for the Spirit to move on him."

We began to pray and ask the Holy Spirit to move. After a few minutes, I noticed Chandler weeping. He tried not to make a big production out of it, but he was unable to conceal it. Soon his cheeks were wet with tears.

"I feel something like electricity all over me," Chandler said, after I asked him what was happening.

"Don't be embarrassed, but I want you to tell us why you are crying. Is it sadness?"

"No. It's love. I am feeling the strongest love I've ever felt."

I had them. There was near silence, except for the guitar I softly strummed.

"For the first half of my life, I labored under the belief that I wasn't good enough, that in fact there was something very wrong with me, something that would keep me from finding my place in the world. I believed I had to perform to be loved, and I thought God looked at me the same way. But when I started reaching out to him, God began to heal and bless me. All I did was ask. He will do all these things for each one of you as well. All you have to do is ask."

CHOOSING TO FORGIVE
THE STORY OF ANNA
WRITTEN BY LISA BRADSHAW

My mother always said she would divorce my dad once my brother and I grew up and left the house. She blamed us for their unhappiness and said they'd been happy until we came along.

"When you get married, you might as well wear black instead of white. Your life is over. You'll never have a life of your own after your wedding day," she told me.

I believed her.

In truth, I later concluded, it was my dad's accident at work that killed their marriage. He was disabled and could no longer work, so he was forced to manage our small 10-acre farm of chickens, goats and other small animals and the alfalfa field that helped support it. Sadly, it changed him and it changed them, and it did more damage to their marriage than my brother and I could have ever managed to do.

But I grew up believing that as their firstborn, I held the fate of my parents' marriage in my hands. I wondered how I could ever be anything more than a burden and a disappointment to my mother. I felt trapped. If I left home, my mother would divorce my dad, and I would be to blame. If I stayed, I would never have a life of my own, and I would never have peace.

❧❧❧

I never understood how or why my mother could so easily dismiss all that mattered to me. Never once did she say she had higher hopes for my life than her own. In fact, she continued to blame her children for all that was wrong in her life.

"If I could figure out a way to kill you kids and kill myself without getting caught in between, I would do it," she told me. She threatened to kill herself regularly, but this was the first time she had threatened to kill my brother and me. She wanted to be set free from her miserable life and felt she needed to "save" us, too. Death seemed like the only way out.

We endured more than just harsh words and cruel talk. Sometimes she used a belt or willow switches or cords, as well. It was okay for her to get physical with us, but the two times my dad spanked me, my mother came unglued.

"You are never to lay a hand on them!" she barked at him ferociously. "You're just like my dad. All he ever wanted to do was beat on us. Don't you dare touch them ever again!"

It made no sense for her to stand up for us like that, but little did when it came to my mother. I eventually came to the conclusion that she was not protecting us from my dad. She just wanted to control everything, including who beat us and when we were beaten.

One time, my mother had my brother and me trapped

under the kitchen table, wildly swinging her belt at us, in her rage not caring where or how hard the blows fell.

"Come out from under there!" she shrieked, her anger rising with every swish of her belt.

We sat helpless and huddled under the table. The two of us clung to one another, wailing and quaking in fear.

"You'd better stop!" my dad demanded.

"You stay out of it!" she screamed.

"You're going to make them bleed!" he bellowed back.

For some reason, the idea of making us bleed stopped her in her tracks, and she stopped suddenly, leaving us alone and confused under the kitchen table.

"Come on," my brother said, as we quietly and slowly came out from under the table.

My dad being home all the time seemed to keep my mother's anger in check. I only remember her flying into a rage three times, and each time, my brother and I ended up on the receiving end of her anger. We quickly learned it was much wiser not to provoke her.

❧❧❧

I grew up going to church with friends and neighbors. My parents never went with me. It was something I sought on my own. Church was a safe, peaceful place away from the condemnation of my mother, and I went willingly.

My mother never supported the idea. When she was a child, my mother and her siblings went to church with a neighbor who actually told them they had no chance of getting to heaven.

"You're going straight to hell!" the neighbor told my mother. "There's no place for you in heaven!"

My mother told me she was raised to believe she wasn't good enough for God.

"I was dirty and undeserving."

Why she tried to pass the same onto me, I never understood.

Despite her efforts, I did not share my mother's feelings and continued going to Sunday school. When I was 16, I regularly drove myself to church and made the decision to get baptized.

"I think you should wait to get baptized. It's not a wise thing to do." First, my mom discouraged. "You don't know what you are getting yourself into."

Then her tone intensified. "No. I don't want you to get baptized!" she said loudly and firmly.

I had to sneak out of the house to attend church. With my mother vehemently opposed to my faith, I became even more committed to God and his place in my life.

All of that changed when my parents decided to move us from Idaho to Oklahoma. I did not want to go.

"You don't even care about my going to college!" I yelled. "How will I ever make something of myself in a small town in Oklahoma? There isn't even a college there!"

"You'll make new friends. You'll figure it out," they told me, negating all my plans for a formal college education.

When we arrived, and it was as bad as I had feared, I

completely rebelled. I started drinking and doing drugs and partying with new like-minded friends. I started sleeping around with guys my age and older. All plans I'd envisioned for my future before the move started to fade away, and God became the furthest person from my mind.

I did my best to get in enough trouble and cause enough problems to get sent back home to Idaho to live with my grandmother, but my efforts weren't working. No matter how much trouble I caused, my parents refused to send me back.

I even wondered if getting pregnant would push my parents far enough.

"Mom, what would you do if I got pregnant?"

"Well, Anna, I'd disown you and kick you out on the street," she answered without hesitation.

"Well, I'd get an abortion, and you'd never even know about it," I sharply replied.

She made no response and continued peeling potatoes at the kitchen sink.

❧❧❧

I continued on my rebellious path, trying to get sent back to Idaho to live with my grandmother, when a chance appointment with my dentist provided my only hope for returning.

We had not yet established a dentist in Oklahoma, and I needed my wisdom teeth pulled, so my parents let me go back to Idaho to have it done. I packed two duffle bags full of everything I could squeeze in them, got on a bus and headed for my grandmother's house.

After my dental procedure, I never returned to Oklahoma. I was 19 years old and stayed with my grandmother for a few months before getting a job in a small town nearby. I was finally free.

I was less wild upon my return to Idaho. I was never addicted to the drugs and alcohol and the partying lifestyle that I participated in while in Oklahoma. It was strictly social and largely about rebelling against my mother. I was still determined to do whatever I wanted whenever I wanted.

I knew during that time I was rebelling against God as well, but I also felt like I could go back to God when I was done having fun. I remember telling God, "If you really cared about me, you would send me someone to take me to church."

❧❧❧

Living in Idaho, I finally got my act together. I went to school, just as I had always wanted, and became a licensed practical nurse (LPN). Things were looking up.

Then, a year after finishing school, I had female-related health problems and was told by my doctor that I probably would not be able to have children. I had always dreamed of being a mother one day — the kind of mother I never had. My infertility was another blow in my life's plan, so I once again fell into my old pattern of self-sabotage and took the rebellious path. I became even more promiscuous than I had been in the past, drowning my sorrows in the arms of an endless string of men.

I threw out my birth control of choice and slept around without a care about getting pregnant since the chances were so slim — slim, but not impossible.

Soon, I discovered I was pregnant, but I had slept with so many men that I did not know who the father was, and I did not care to figure it out.

My mother had finally divorced my dad and was then living back in Idaho. I went to tell her the news, hoping in vain for some maternal support.

"You're far too young to have a child," she answered sharply. "You can barely take care of yourself."

"Maybe I should just have an abortion," I suggested hesitantly.

"Well, if that's what you want to do, go ahead," she replied flatly.

That was the end of our discussion on the topic.

She never flat out told me to have an abortion. She did everything but make the suggestion herself. Instead, she filled me with doubt and shame for getting in the predicament and made sure I knew she would not be helping me with a baby conceived out of wedlock, as if she had ever cared to lead me down a righteous path.

Five days before my 24th birthday, I chose to have an abortion and end the pregnancy. I went with a friend who had already had a few abortions, and the way she had described the procedure and how she felt afterward, it did not seem like such a big deal. I went in thinking I would not be affected by it much at all. Many women I knew had had abortions, and they seemed to be doing just fine.

It was not until the drive home from the clinic that the truth about what I had done began to really sink in. Something I had done so carelessly began to weigh heavily on my soul. I sat stone-faced and motionless in the car. I felt completely hollow, like a fragile shell sitting where a woman had once been. But at the same time, I felt the rising of overwhelming grief and sadness threatening to drown me as it poured over my body.

My baby. My baby. My baby, I kept saying in my head. *I killed my baby.*

That night, I lay clutching myself in my bed and weeping for the life I had killed. I considered the oath I had taken as a nurse, to protect life, and knew I had failed. I considered how I had let God down and feared that this time I had gone too far. It had always been my intention to return to God, but how could he still love me after what I had done?

✎✎✎✎

I was in and out of relationships for the next six years. Living in a self-destructive haze, I went back to drugs and alcohol and found myself in the beds of many men. Nothing eased my depression or quenched the pain. God no longer seemed an option for me because I had betrayed him by murdering my baby. I saw no way out of the ongoing cycle of depression and regret.

By the time I turned 30, I met a man with a 4-year-old son. I fell in love with both Jake and his son Andy. And while the destructive pattern eventually ended, the depression continued. I just could not stop wondering, in the presence of Andy and in the absence of the baby I had aborted, what my own child would be like by then.

Within a year, I was pregnant again, and although this child was also unplanned, I knew having an abortion was no longer an option for me, with or without Jake and Andy.

"I won't have another abortion," I informed Jake. "I'll have this baby alone if I have to, but I won't have another abortion."

"We'll do it together," he assured me. "We'll have the baby together."

I felt guilty for the choices I had made, including choosing to bring our baby into the world out of wedlock, as well as my continued guilt about killing my first baby.

The moment my daughter was born, I felt amazed at the love that poured out of me and how much love I felt from her in return. As I held her in my arms, I made a little wish, that there would be no trace of my mother's cruelty in how I loved my own daughter.

When we had a private moment, after Jake had left to take Andy home, I professed my love to Isabelle and began to wonder what it would be like to forgive myself for killing her brother or sister six years earlier.

"Oh, sweet girl. You are so perfect and beautiful. I don't deserve you," I whispered to her through tears thick with maternal longing. "I will do my best to raise you up right and teach you all that I know. And, hopefully, you won't make the same mistakes I have made. I don't want you to have a life of regrets."

My heart burned with each word of this promise to my beloved daughter.

As I spoke these words to Isabelle, I knew with every fiber of my being that I had major work to do in *my own* heart if I ever wanted to give her the life I was promising her. But how could I change my heart and life without God? I still felt certain he would not forgive me.

ॐॐॐ

I wondered about my other baby even more after Isabelle's birth. The depression lingered and increased. Meanwhile, Andy started attending church with his friend's parents. When they came by to pick up Andy, they would come inside to visit for a few minutes. Little did I know they were praying for us.

When Isabelle was 3 years old, I started experiencing irrational behavior. I was having mood swings, and the littlest things would set me off into a tailspin of furious tears. It would go on for days, then stop for a while, only to start up again without warning.

"What's wrong with you, Anna?" Jake shouted in frustration. "I never know who you are from one day to the next!"

"You think that's bad? I start my morning not knowing who I am going to be that day!" I raged back.

"You're impossible. There is no pleasing you." He threw up his arms, completely exasperated.

"Well, you never help with Isabelle," I accused, pointing my finger right in his face. "I do everything myself!"

"I babysit her every time you ask me to do it," he spat defensively.

"It's not *babysitting* when she's your own DAUGHTER!" I shrieked with clenched fists.

He did not have an answer, but I could see the end was near. We both could see it. Not only was our relationship failing, but I was feeling more and more guilt for raising Isabelle in a home with a man I had no intention of marrying.

"Just leave! Get out of here!" I commanded. "I can't be nice today."

I cried when he left. I was completely out of control, sobbing and crying out for my dead baby. I called out to God, fearing I was losing my mind, unable to gain control.

"Please, God," I begged. "Save me from this torment."

I was at the end of my rope. I knew my daughter needed me and deserved more than I was giving her. I was not keeping the promise I made to her the day she was born. I was not raising her right. I was not doing my best to give her what she needed.

As I cried out to God, I suddenly remembered the stories Andy told me after Sunday school. Then I started reading some of the little stories and papers he'd brought home. As I read each word of God's love and his promise to forgive and make us whole again, I knew my only hope was to return to him. I knew he was my only way out of the deep, dark hole I had dug for myself since the day I chose to abort my baby.

The very next Sunday, I attended Harvest Church with Andy and his friend's parents. As I sat in the church pew and was met by the smiles of those around me, it reminded me of my prayer all those years before when I first moved to Oklahoma, telling God if he really cared about me, he would send someone to bring me to church.

I immediately started praying for God to help find a home for Isabelle and me. Jake and I weren't married, and I didn't want to live with him like that anymore. I needed strength to leave him and start anew on my own with Isabelle.

It took almost a year, but the time came for us to go. God answered my prayers. He gave me the strength and ability to leave Jake once and for all.

"I can't live here with you anymore," I told Jake. "But you can have whatever relationship and time with Isabelle that you want as her father."

Though Jake did not maintain a relationship with Isabelle, I believe that leaving him was the best thing for both of us. God was building our new life, with himself at the center.

೫೫೫

I continued on my path to healing. God began to show me people in my life who I needed to forgive. He helped me realize that I, too, needed the same forgiveness I was learning to extend to others. Each time I was wronged and exercised forgiveness, or each time I thought back to my mother's ways when I was a child, the idea of forgiveness began to mount as I moved closer to what God had in store for me at Harvest Church.

Harvest Church experienced a time of renewal and refreshing of our faith for the next three years. During that time, we had weekly prayer meetings that started at 7 p.m. and sometimes went on until after midnight. During the meetings, people were given visions or words of knowledge, healing took place and, on Sundays, church attendance increased.

During that time, I experienced much spiritual, mental, emotional and physical healing in my own life. It was as if God came into my heart and mind through the events at Harvest Church and scrubbed every inch of me clean. I felt like he wiped away the pain and lies of my childhood, the emotional turmoil and depression I struggled with for years, and made me whole, an entirely new person — the woman I was meant to be. I had come to know God as my heavenly father, and I fell in love with Jesus, but one thing continued to haunt me.

I still cried when people talked about abortion. I felt a deep and penetrating embarrassment and condemnation — as a murderer of my own baby. I found it hard to believe that God could love me unconditionally.

It was not until Harvest Church sponsored Cleansing Streams Ministries workshop classes, and I attended a conference at Vineyard Church in Boise, Idaho, that I learned through those teachings to forgive myself for the abortion. The conference was a conclusion to the Cleansing Streams Ministries teachings. We applied the weeks of lessons as an exercise in freeing ourselves from the past so that God could set us free to walk forward in the plans he had for our future with many prayers of repentance and forgiveness. It allowed God to break the bondage of our pasts.

At one point during the three-day intense teachings, I spoke about my abortion and not ever truly knowing who the father was. As part of the healing process, in front of women I would likely never see again, each of us listed all of the men we had slept with and prayed for forgiveness from each man for being promiscuous with them.

Each of us prayed our own prayer of repentance. For me, my prayer of forgiveness was for my abortion.

Father, I thank you, Jesus, for forgiving me and my sins. I pray for your forgiveness for having an abortion and killing my unborn child.

One exercise in particular was especially powerful for me. It was during a time of prayer when we were instructed to clap as we prayed aloud. The clapping helped to signify freedom from the burdens of our past. We all stood together, each experiencing complete release from the stronghold of our sins, one by one.

"In the name of Jesus, I break …" we each said, then

clapped our hands and finished our statements. "… I have been set free from a murderous spirit!"

Each of us said the prayer together, clapped together and listened and shared as we spoke of breaking the bondage of sin, each of us feeling set free of the sin we had not managed to forgive ourselves for before the conference that weekend.

It was the repetition of the message and the power of clapping out the sin during prayer that eventually permeated my heart. Surrounded by such abundant forgiveness, I could no longer deny God's love for me. God wanted me to forgive myself, knowing it was the only way I would really come to serve him with an open heart, free from the blame and shame I placed on myself every moment of every day since having the abortion.

I finally allowed myself to consider that with God's love came the promise I would one day see my child again, in the perfection of the heavenly home God provided for my baby. It was not my reason for choosing God, but I felt certain it was a result of choosing him.

ॐॐॐ

Our pastor at Harvest Church spoke often of forgiveness. When he talked about teaching a person how to forgive someone else, he suggested these words: "Because Jesus has forgiven me, I choose to forgive."

I used these words to forgive those who wronged me, and I finally began using them to forgive myself.

I started repeating these words to myself daily: "Because Jesus has forgiven me, I choose to forgive myself, and I know, one day, I will be reunited with my baby in heaven."

Eventually, I began to believe the words that led to my own healing.

≈≈≈

Part of my healing also came when I felt God telling me that I needed to share my experience. I ignored this calling for years until I took a college speech class and our professor asked us to speak on something we felt passionate about. I chose to speak about Post Abortion Stress Disorder (PASD), which was something I had been studying for a few years before choosing it as my topic.

"Look to your left, then look to your right," I told each person in the class. "One of the two people sitting next to you has been affected by abortion. My daughter knows the truth about her unborn brother or sister, and she has had to face her own grief because of it. Abortion does not just affect the mother. It affects the father, the grandparents, the children who would have had a sibling and the many people who will never know the love of the child who was aborted."

Abortion is complicated and painful and can bring with it a difficult path to peace and forgiveness. But there is a path. And the closer we are to God, the better lit our path will be.

CHOOSING TO FORGIVE

I have never forgotten giving my speech in class and how it allowed me to publicly profess my sin of abortion in an effort to help others.

It was the first step in allowing me to help others see the damage abortion does, bringing the healing through God that I have experienced personally.

In the process of researching and speaking about PASD that first time, I learned about women who experienced the guilt and suffering of abortion but did not find the saving grace of God. Many women never truly faced the heartache of having an abortion until the emotions were triggered by a specific event, like the birth of another child or when an aborted child would have celebrated a milestone, such as a birthday or graduation. They did not have a path to peace and forgiveness for the choice to have an abortion.

I began to feel even more grateful to God for never leaving me, even when I made the conscious decision to leave him.

He has blessed me beyond belief. My daughter is a living reminder of God's love and forgiveness, even when I didn't deserve it.

He gave her to me, even though I made mistakes, and for that unconditional, undeserved kindness, I will be forever grateful.

≈≈≈

Not long after I gave my PASD speech and shared my story, I was visiting with a woman named Amy. Shortly before our visit, she had opened her heart to Jesus and became a Christian. I just felt moved by God to tell Amy I had had an abortion, like it was important for her to know.

"When I was 24, I had an abortion," I said suddenly.

Amy looked shocked by my confession, yet open to hearing about it.

"So did I," she confessed. "I was just a teenager. I've never forgiven myself."

I told Amy about the prayer of forgiveness.

As Jesus has forgiven me, I choose to forgive myself.

"Amy, you don't have to feel guilt, shame or embarrassment about it anymore. God has forgiven you. It's gone. Now, because he has forgiven you, you can forgive yourself. You don't have to carry this anymore. You're free."

Amy's face lit up as she realized the truth of my words, that a path to complete freedom and forgiveness was before her.

We prayed together.

As Jesus has forgiven me, I choose to forgive myself for my abortion.

With each word spoken, Amy was set free. When we were done, she cried tears of joy.

"Thank you, Anna," she said, "for helping me find my way. I never knew I could feel such forgiveness, acceptance and love."

As she declared her newfound freedom, I thanked God. *Thank you for loving me so much, for showing me how something so bad can be used for good, for teaching me how to forgive, for never giving up on me and for giving me such peace.*

RISING FROM THE ASHES
THE STORY OF JASON
WRITTEN BY JOY STEINER MOORE

Red-hot flames shot high into the air, filling the sky above my backyard with thick black smoke. It felt like a bad dream — a horrid nightmare.

I have to fight this!

Adrenaline surged through my body as I hurried to the garden hose and cranked it on. But as I aimed it in the direction of my burning shop and saw the weak spray turn to mist, I knew I was fighting a losing battle.

Sirens blared in the distance, telling me help was on the way.

They'll be too late.

The flames danced from the shop to the garage, scorching the wall of the house just a few feet away. I couldn't just stand there and watch. Steeling myself against the heat, I ran into the blaze to save whatever I could.

"Jason, get out of there!" my wife screamed from the safety of the driveway as I came out of the shop dragging one of my irreplaceable saddles. I dropped it on the driveway and headed back into the wall of thick black smoke pouring out of the door for the next load. Time after time I returned to the shop, to the garage and to my office, rescuing bits and pieces of our lives — saddles, equipment, tools, my computer — anything I could grab quickly without putting my life on the line.

The heat was unbearable, and I felt it blistering my face. My side and chest ached from the broken ribs I'd suffered the day before, but I limped along, anyway, determined to fight the fire before it completely ravaged my property and my home.

Within minutes, emergency vehicles arrived — 17 in all — and I was ordered to stay back, away from the danger. I felt sick to my stomach. As much as I wished it were just a bad dream, it was all too real. Within minutes, our pleasant Sunday afternoon had turned into complete and utter terror.

I was running back and forth helping the firemen in any way I could, answering questions and dragging hoses. I finally stopped for a moment and stood silently with my wife and kids, wiping beads of sweat from my forehead, and watched as everything I'd worked for turned to ashes in front of my eyes. I was already $300,000 in debt, with bankruptcy on the horizon and our house and property scheduled for auction. This fire felt like the final nail in my coffin, taking with it every scrap of my business, my only means of livelihood.

What am I going to do now?

&&&

"The breast cancer has been removed, but to be perfectly frank with you, it can and may come back," the doctor told my mom. "It might make a difference with how you want to live your life."

I was only 5 at the time, so of course I was thrilled when my parents decided to give up city life in Portland and buy a cattle ranch a couple hours away in the country. They were looking for a peaceful lifestyle where they could live their dreams. I just loved the idea of being a cowboy.

Life was good for a while. Our family was happy and stable, and I learned the value of hard work. We went to church on Sundays and got involved in our small rural community. Our home life was extremely peaceful. In 1983, Mom's cancer came back. Dad sold the cattle and decided to go into the sheep business. He figured it would be easier with my sisters grown and gone, leaving him with a little boy and a sick wife to care for on his own.

Powel Butte was a cattleman's area and not very hospitable for sheep, so we moved to Madras where Dad used his construction background to remodel the ranch accordingly.

Mom's second cancer diagnosis was a death sentence in the form of a brain tumor. My mom fought hard for four years, but in the end, she was drained and tired. She passed away when I was 12.

Suddenly, it was just Dad and me on the ranch. Saddened by the loss of my mom, I started to do my own thing when I wasn't with my dad, and soon I was drinking and hanging out with the cool crowd. I lived two separate lives. I was one person at home with Dad and a completely different person at school.

My older cousin Pete came to live with us off and on for a few years, and his exciting, fast-paced life enthralled me. He was my hero. He and I drank and had a lot of fun together, especially when my dad decided to start his construction business in the city, leaving me in charge of the ranch during the week, with the occasional neighbor checking in. I knew how to keep up appearances. I put on a pretty good façade, so nobody suspected the continuous trouble I was getting myself into.

৵৵৵

"Pete! Pete! Open up!" I rapped on the door of his old broken-down apartment one morning around 10.

I knew he was home because his jeep was parked out front. When he answered, he invited me in. He quickly tiptoed over to close the bedroom door, but not before I saw a strange, barely dressed woman stretched across his bed. He put his finger to his lips, motioning for me to keep it down. Apparently, the date he'd picked up the night before was still sleeping.

I quickly surveyed the messy living room, littered with empty beer cans and other clutter. The whole scene disgusted me.

I knew some of the women that he would pick up at bars had kids who would come along, but it suddenly hit me with fresh eyes. The thought horrified me. Sure, the kids didn't *live* with him, but I couldn't imagine any child hanging out in that place, ever. Pete cracked open his third beer that morning, shaking me out of my repulsed reverie.

I stood there in the doorway, truly *seeing* my cousin for the first time. I'd never noticed before, but he looked old for his early 20s. Honestly, he was a complete mess.

I thought about the trouble he had keeping a job and paying his bills. And I started connecting the dots. Pete was my idol. But this? This chaos he called a life? This was not how I envisioned my future. I didn't want to be strung out when I was 23. I wanted more for myself.

Quietly, I left his apartment and drove home, lost in my thoughts for almost three hours.

Before then, I had always seen Pete at his best. I'd never seen him in the party's aftermath.

Is all the partying really worth it?

Over the next several days, I replayed the scene of Pete's life over and over again in my mind. The more I thought about it, the sicker I felt. It was depressing. I compared Pete to the men I really respected, like my dad and my grandpa. I knew with all the limited wisdom of my 17 years that my choices were leading me down a path more like Pete's than theirs. I had been raised differently than he had, and I knew better. I had taken my family for granted. The very bed I sat on, that very room and that very house were all a direct result of my dad's hard work and the harmony in our lives. I had been to church hundreds of times in my life, and I understood that, though I had never had much use for God before, a huge difference in my family's peaceful, stable life was due to a belief and trust in him.

A few days later, I was driving my truck and pulled up to a stop sign by a little country store. "God, if you're there," I prayed, "I want to live for you, like Dad does. Like Grandpa and Mom did. I don't want a life like Pete's. Please help me to change. Please help me to start over."

The weight of my decision to change was a heavy burden for my young shoulders. I wanted to change, but I knew that it meant changing my friends, my activities and my general focus in life. That was a pretty big commitment for a kid getting ready to start his senior year in high school. But I had a sudden thought.

"And, God," I added, "if you could please help me meet a nice Christian girl to marry and settle down with, I think I might be able to live this Christian life that you are calling me to live."

༄ༀ༄

Two weeks later, I sat on the heater in the hallway of my high school, talking with friends and waiting for the bell to ring. A group of girls was heading toward us, and one cute girl in particular caught my eye. As Tina walked by, I said, "Hi!" and she smiled and kept on walking. I wanted — no, needed — to get her attention, so I stuck out my foot to trip her just a little as she passed. She stumbled slightly and looked back and smiled.

The bell rang, and we each hurried off to class. Later in the day, in my agriculture class, Tina ended up sitting right in front of me. I spent the next few days teasing her and trying to get on her good side. It took some wooing, but I was eventually successful. We went to a dance together later that week and began dating immediately after.

And that is how I met my wife.

જ જ જ

I started working for Les Schwab Tires shortly after meeting Tina. My dad taught me construction on the side. Eventually, I got my general contractor's license and started building houses for a living.

Tina and I got married when we were 19 and 20, and since my contracting business was just getting off the ground, things were tight financially.

One September Sunday, just a month after we'd gotten married, Tina and I sat in our little country church. We didn't have much money, but when the offering plate was passed, I opened up my wallet and dropped in a whopping $35 cash. It was quite a stretch for us, but it just felt like the right thing to do.

When we got home, I noticed that the widow lady across the street had lost some shingles off her roof. I grabbed my hammer and ladder and climbed up on her roof to nail them back on for her.

"Oh, thank you so much, Jason!" the neighbor exclaimed gratefully, as I headed back down the ladder.

"It's no big deal." I smiled. "Happy to help." After all, it had only taken 15 minutes.

"Well, here." She pressed a small envelope in my hand.

When I was back in my garage across the street, I tore open the envelope to find a thank-you note and $35, the exact amount I had dropped in the offering plate an hour before.

My eyes widened. She could have given me $20, or another nice even number like $30 or $40. But I believe God made sure she gave me exactly $35, just to prove a point that he always takes care of us — to make sure I understood that he was involved in every detail of my life. I didn't know it then, but that was a lesson I would need repeated over and over again as I grew older and the stakes got higher.

෨෨෨

Over the next couple of years, I worked extremely hard to attain that stable, harmonious lifestyle I'd always dreamed of. The stress of my business weighed heavily on me, and I wasn't always the easiest person to live with. As Tina and I became parents, the pressure only magnified, and I became deeply depressed. Tina tried to help me stay positive and encouraged me to ask God for help, but there wasn't much she could say to help. It was really between me and God.

I had noticed that I would go through periods of happiness and peace, followed by periods of deep darkness. It was a continuous cycle. One month I would feel like God cared for me because of something amazing I experienced, but then, as time went on, I would forget and sink into depression again. I was tired of the roller coaster ride.

When our son Tyler was just a few months old, I was at a real low point. In fact, that particular period of depression lasted for six months. I couldn't find words to explain the darkness. All I knew was that it hovered over me, and it wasn't right.

Tina and I sat in our little church one Sunday, nestled in the back row. The communion plate was being passed, and I paused to decide whether or not I should participate. First Corinthians 11:27-29 came to mind, where the Bible clearly instructs that we are to examine our hearts before taking communion. The crackers and grape juice were only to be taken by those who had accepted God's forgiveness for the things they had done wrong — who believed they had been cleansed and made new by belief in Jesus, God's son. I struggled with such darkness that I didn't know what I believed anymore. I certainly didn't feel close to God.

The person next to me handed me the tray, and I quickly passed it on to Tina without taking any.

She cast me a sideways glance but didn't say anything. She understood that communion was a personal decision.

But in my heart, I ached. I ached to feel better in my mind, to feel happy again. I ached to be free of the darkness and the icy fingers of depression.

My heart is sick, and I can't fix it!

While they were finishing passing out communion, I squeezed my eyes shut and cried a silent prayer for help.

God, I don't want to feel this way anymore. Please heal my heart. Only you can fix it!

I pictured myself holding my heart up to God with both my hands, offering it to him.

Just then, an elderly man from the other side of the church rushed to the front of the room and set his communion tray down on the podium.

"God gave me a vision," he said. "There is a man here who has come to the Lord many times but not completely crossed over. You need to come forward so we can pray with you." I had grown up in church, and I had never seen anything like this.

Oh, no.

I thought I might be sick. The man's words described me perfectly. How many times had I had every intention of changing my life and simply skirted along the surface, just barely getting by? I had toyed with religion and had worked hard to play the part. But it didn't come easy for me. No matter how many times God intervened in my life, I couldn't seem to hang on to that hope for more than a few weeks or months. I could never quite *cross over.*

The congregation of 70 people waited silently. When nobody responded, a couple of men awkwardly cleared their throats. I started sweating bullets.

Finally, a young man stood up and walked to the front, his head hung low. I relaxed and breathed a small sigh of relief.

"Thank you for coming," the older man said to him. "We'll pray for you, but you're not the one."

A chill of anxiety passed through me, and I felt weak in the knees. Perspiration dripped down my sides, and tears ran down my cheeks. I reached up a hand to wipe it away.

"Jason, honey, are you okay?" Tina whispered.

"No," I rasped.

"Is it you?"

"Yes." I pretty much choked the word out.

"Well, you need to go forward," she urged, squeezing my knee.

"I can't. My legs won't work."

I was so terrified and shaken that I just could not go forward.

The man at the front spoke again after a long time. "It's okay. I know who you are, and we will pray for you where you are sitting." And they did. Trembling from head to toe, I asked God to heal my heart as my church prayed, though they did not know it was for me.

When the service was over, the pastor stood in the back as we filed out the door. When I reached him, I broke down. We went into his office and prayed together. Right there in my pastor's office, I closed my eyes and felt a drastic change happening within me. For once, it wasn't me trying to make the change. God was melting my heart, and all I could do was weep. I began to have a love in my heart that I had never before experienced.

How do you explain a warm, sunny day to someone who has never been outside a cold, dark prison cell? I had never before experienced such personal life change as I did the weeks and months and years to follow. A song at church would bring me to tears. I felt a love for my wife and child in a whole new way that ran deep. I began to have a love for people that surpassed all understanding and a peace that God held me and my life in his hands.

My life could no longer be all about me and what I wanted. It had to be about others. Instead of being obsessed with creating my own success and my own stable life, I needed to focus on *God's* plan. I had been trying too hard for so long, when all God really wanted was my whole heart and then for me to let him take care of the rest.

❧❧❧

Each year in the winter and early spring, my business slowed down significantly. I almost looked forward to those times because it allowed me to study the Bible more deeply and really work on my relationship with God. The problem was, with no business, there was no money.

How am I going to pay these bills? I thought, as I sat in my office one afternoon. The bank account was drained, and the outlook for potential jobs looked pretty bleak. I wasn't sure how we were going to make it. But it suddenly occurred to me that I should ask God.

"You know all the bills I have here, God," I prayed. "Could you please bring me a job quickly that will pay all my bills? They're due next we —"

My prayer was interrupted by the ringing of the telephone. I just stared at it dumbly for a second. The business phone hadn't rung in three months. Irritated at the interruption in my prayer time, I answered the phone.

"Hi, Jason," a woman greeted me. "You came out and looked at my roof a year ago, but now I'm in a situation where I need it done as soon as possible. Do you think you could help me? What's your availability this week?"

My mouth dropped open.

God, you're kidding, right? That was fast!

The lady's re-roof project paid exactly what we needed, and I was able to pay all our bills on time.

❧❧❧

The 2008 recession hit my business hard. I went from having 13 employees to having trouble keeping two or three busy, even through the normally busy summer months. I tried advertising, and I expanded the business into more trades, but it still wasn't enough. I worked hard, but at the end of 2009, we still lost $35,000 and maxed out all the credit cards and our line of credit just to pay the bills, leaving no money or credit left over. On top of that, as we entered January 2010, all my planned projects fell through, so there was no work on the horizon.

At this point, Tina and I had four children — Tyler, twin girls Chloe and Hannah and a 3-year-old son Jack. We had visited some friends' church at Christmastime and felt like that was the church where we were supposed to be going. So after the first of the year, we made the difficult decision to leave all our friends and switch churches. It just so happened that our new church's parsonage was in the middle of being remodeled. We learned that the pastor and his family were living in the home with no insulation or sheetrock on the walls. Since I didn't have any other projects going on, I seemed to be extremely free to donate my time.

"God, you know that we're broke, but I'm going to finish this remodel. It's up to you to provide what we need."

Over the next few months, as I worked on the parsonage, I spent a lot of time on the church property, becoming particularly close to the pastor, as well as a man from Holland — a new Christian believer named Abe.

Abe was visiting friends in Oregon, preparing to withdraw money out of his account to avenge his daughter's murder in Central America, when he ended up at our church and realized he needed Jesus in his life. He had a lot of questions about his new faith. We spent hours together talking, learning and discussing. He had quite a bit of anger and darkness to overcome. He came to the realization that he had to forgive the men who murdered his daughter.

In the meantime, I was experiencing complete financial meltdown. Throughout that summer, as my own business failed to bring in projects and I was, again, $30,000 behind in bills, I felt that though I was at a spiritual high, the other half of my life was in ruins. The dichotomy was mind-boggling to me. I believed I was doing what I was supposed to be doing, but it certainly wasn't paying off. And yet I knew that Jesus said, "Seek first the kingdom of God and his righteousness, and all these things will be added unto you."

I believed that my investment in the church parsonage and in Abe's life were of utmost importance. I had to also believe that God would take care of the bills somehow.

❧❧❧

In August, my friend Chuck and I took Abe to the coast for a weekend, so he could experience the joys of crabbing. We dropped off three crab pots near the mouth of the Alsea River. Then we cruised inland in our 13-foot aluminum boat and dropped three more pots in the river. When we returned to the first group of pots, they were washing out to sea on a strong outgoing tide.

Chuck was at the helm and yelled, "Go get 'em, Jason."

"Really? Are they worth it?" I replied warily. "Oh, okay."

As I gave the throttle a twist and began driving out to sea into the big waves, I started to get a little scared.

"Hand me a lifejacket!" I yelled frantically to my friends. I froze, utterly petrified, realizing how easy it would be to capsize with just the right wave. I'd heard many stories on the news over the prior five years or so of people who had lost their lives in this exact situation in the exact same place.

As I started to put on the lifejacket, I realized that, should we capsize, a lifejacket would do me no good. I dropped it on the floor of the boat.

I realized that we were going way past the safe waters of the river and out into the Pacific Ocean. The only thing between us and the big sea was the loud breakers, where the ocean waves met the river current.

I knew there was only one thing to do.

"Lord Jesus!" I cried to heaven. "Keep us safe! Please, watch over us!"

A peace washed over me. *Okay, I've done my business with God. Now let's roll!*

We went out within 50 yards or so of the jaws (where the river meets the ocean, way out from the mouth of the river) when we turned around in the 4-foot-high waves. As we struggled against the white caps, we recovered two of the three crab pots and were on our way back in when the motor ran out of gas. Suddenly, we were adrift in the bay, with no motor and no control over our direction in a strong outgoing current. We were doomed, drifting out to sea toward those deafening breaker waves.

Oh, no. What do we do now?

I handed Chuck an old skinny wooden oar, the only one we had.

"You start rowing, and I'll shake the gas can and see if we can get anything going in the engine."

In the meantime, I kept praying. I began calling on the Lord loudly.

"LORD JESUS, SAVE US! LORD, HELP US!"

I didn't look up until we were crashing through the breaker waves at the shore.

We glided to safety in the midst of treacherous

conditions. Abe jumped from the boat and began excitedly explaining that, as we prayed, it felt like a hand was pushing on his back, gently guiding the boat across the river current to the ocean shore.

"God just pushed us to shore!" Abe grinned from ear to ear. His excitement was uncontainable. "God just pushed us to shore!"

"That's exactly what he did," I agreed, shaking my head in amazement.

As we drove back home, I said to Abe, "I feel like God is telling me that the waves in Holland are going to be pretty big, but you need to know you can always call on the Lord."

Abe was still grinning, and I knew that God was still at work in his heart. This was a miracle he wouldn't forget for quite a while. He was wound as tight as a clock about that event for days.

❧❧❧

Tina and I were still sinking financially, so we made an appointment with a bankruptcy attorney for Friday, September 3. The very thought of going bankrupt made me sick, but I didn't know what else to do.

"Well, you're not bankrupt yet," our attorney said, looking over his glasses at the reports laid out on his grand desk. "But my advice is to sell everything that you own that you would lose, anyway, and try to get through the recession as far as you can. When you do go bankrupt, you'll keep your furniture and one vehicle. There is nothing you can do about your house being auctioned on December 5. You might be able to make it two or three years before you go bankrupt."

I sat there in my chair, feeling absolutely defeated. I felt like a complete failure. My dad had always trained me to pay my bills, and until then, I always had. Going bankrupt made me feel like I was losing my integrity. I knew it was out of my control; however, I couldn't help the feeling of guilt. Where did I go wrong, and what would I do? Building had been my life for so long. I tried so hard to stay successful at life, and I was ending up worse than I ever imagined.

You're going to lose everything. Make peace with it.

The only good thing we came away with from that meeting was knowing what to expect in the months to follow. We walked out of the office, hand in hand, our heads hung low.

The next day, a Saturday, I took Abe up into the mountains to go horse packing — an activity I loved doing with people. Long before, I had sold my snowmobiles and invested in horses and gear because they were cheaper and kept the cowboy inside me alive and well.

I'm going to have to sell the horses, too, I thought to myself, as we traveled through a beautiful valley, surrounded by gorgeous mountainous landscape. It made me sad because I'd found that horse packing was a great way to get people out into nature — and especially to reach out to people like Abe.

I had trained several horses before and normally bounced pretty well when I hit the ground, but that day I didn't. Everything happened so quickly. By the time we descended from the mountains, I was nursing a few broken ribs. I guess I should have been content in avoiding the creek instead of attempting to make the young colt cross over it.

Wow, this certainly hasn't been the best couple of days, I thought wryly.

At church the following morning, Abe tracked me down to check on me.

"Jason, how are you feeling?" he asked, concerned.

"Sore." I laughed half-heartedly.

"Well, I have something for you," Abe continued, reaching into his backpack. "Maybe this movie will make you feel better."

He handed me a DVD titled *The Pineapple Story.*

The cover featured a photograph of a thatched roof hut, surrounded by palm trees. It looked like a children's movie from the 70s.

"The kids will like it, too," Abe said, winking.

"Thanks." I smiled, grateful for Abe's genuine, unwavering friendship.

❦❦❦

The gist of *The Pineapple Story,* as my kids and I found out that afternoon, was a story about a missionary who had trouble with the local people stealing pineapples from his garden. He was tired of fighting it, so he told God that he could have the garden. He was done with it. As it turned out, the people stealing the pineapples began to get sick from the pineapples they stole until eventually they stopped taking them once and for all. With a sudden abundance of pineapples in his garden, the missionary found himself in a fruitful pineapple business and was even able to export the fruit, which, in turn, helped fund his ministry to the local people.

So God takes care of our gardens better than we do. He takes care of our stuff better than we can.

The movie ended, and I went outside.

"Okay, God, I get it," I said to him as I leaned against the hitching rail outside my office. "Everything I own is yours. I'm certainly not doing very well with it. I'm going to lose it all, anyway, so you might as well have it."

I hobbled around the shop for a bit, taking care of a few chores here and there, then went back into the house to see what my family was up to. The kids had started the movie again because my wife had awakened from her afternoon nap, and they wanted her to see it.

I sank down onto the couch next to Tina and took her hand in mine.

"It's a good movie," I whispered in her ear.

"That's what I hear," she said, smiling back.

A few minutes later, we heard a loud commotion outside. I looked out the window and saw a car stopped in front of our house. The driver was out of the car, frantically motioning to another passerby.

"What's going on?" Tina asked, coming up behind me.

"I don't know," I answered, heading for the door. As soon as I opened it, I saw what it was all about.

"Fire!" I screamed at the top of my lungs.

"Oh, my gosh! Oh, no!" Tina yelled. "Kids!"

Panic ensued, and our four kids popped up off the floor and scrambled with Tina out to the road.

Our shop was engulfed in flames, and the garage and office were going to be next, I knew.

I felt helpless standing there, trying to fight the flames with a simple garden hose. There was nothing I could do to overpower the fire, which was quickly destroying everything we owned.

Despite my sore broken ribs, I started saving what I could. I ran in and out of the buildings, grabbing whatever was handy and valuable, until at last the firefighters pulled me away, and I stood in the smoky afternoon air watching my life disintegrate into ashes.

જ⊸જ⊸જ

Though our house was structurally saved, the smoke damage was too much. It was not livable. We moved our family into a 27-foot camper. Friends came and helped us sort through the soot, and they helped us clean and repair what we could. We made a list for our insurance company of everything we'd lost.

Not a day went by that we didn't receive several phone calls from creditors. I didn't know how to respond. What do you say when you're standing in a camper, looking out the window at the burn pile that used to be your garage, shop, office and a charred house that is unlivable?

How am I going to pay you when I literally live in a pile of ashes? I had no words.

We were upside down on our house since the recession had killed the housing market. We were living in our camper and in debt up to our eyeballs. I didn't know whether to go to work and try to make money or start fixing up this house that was scheduled to go up for auction in a few months. Where would the money come from?

Church members took care of our tangible needs. They brought us food, and one couple even gave us a check that allowed us to buy groceries. But the tension in our home mounted, and Tina and I argued over stupid things — like potato peelers. Some of our fights were so bad that she called our pastor to come and intervene.

"God, we were watching that movie!" I cried out to him one night after a particularly bad argument. I collapsed on the burn pile on the backside of our property. "I said you could have it all! And then just an hour later, you let it burn to the ground. What's that all about?"

I felt utterly broken and defeated. Heaviness hung in the air, and I felt myself sinking into the darkness, becoming one with the ashes. I'd tried so hard to build a good family and to build a prosperous business.

I cried out to God. "Even if I lose everything, I will still praise you. Even if you crush me, yet will I praise you." I wept bitterly and once again surrendered my life to him. My world was completely falling apart.

Tears began to fall from my eyes, and my body shook with sobs.

At 2 a.m., my good friend Chuck came out to look for me. He and Tina had been waiting up, and they were concerned when I didn't return to the camper.

Chuck knew there was nothing to be said. There weren't any answers, and we didn't know what God was doing. So he just sat with me and let me cry, and he asked God to give me peace.

I had served God long enough to know that he could take bad things and work them together for our good. That was difficult for me to remember right then, but I still trusted him. It seemed like my entire life I had been facing insurmountable obstacles, and my relationship with God was always up and down. There were times where he felt close, and there were times where he felt distant. It seemed like I always had to go back and remember the miraculous things he had done in the past — those small acts that had built my faith in him from the ground up. And as low as I felt right then, I remembered those miracles and knew in my heart that God was still *good*.

Even if I lose everything, I will still serve him and worship him.

I had just begun teaching a children's group at the church, and in light of everything we were going through, I didn't think I could handle it. My plate was too full for that kind of commitment. But when Tina and I were talking about backing out, a missionary that we barely knew called and encouraged me to stick with it.

"Sometimes when we're doing God's will, the devil tries to attack us," he said. "There's nothing the devil would like to see more than your failure and your inability to reach these kids with Jesus' love. You have to tell him, in the name of Jesus, to leave you alone."

I was told that several times over the following weeks by many pastors and friends. The advice was good for every part of our lives. When Tina and I fought, we began to recognize it as the devil trying to weasel his way between us and split us up.

We told him to get out of our home, in the name of Jesus. "Satan, you have no authority over me or my family. In the name of Jesus, you must go!"

We clung together in that little camper, overwhelmed by the unexplainable peace of God. Our struggles were far from resolved, but we experienced a deeper sense of peace and unity than we ever had in our 15 years of marriage. And the church kids had an extremely dedicated group leader that year — a bankrupt, unemployed man living in a camper, whose only qualification was that he loved and served Jesus.

❧❧❧

We were underinsured, but the insurance payout for our property loss ended up allowing us to settle our debts. We didn't replace anything we'd lost because we used the amount to completely settle all of our debts. We decided that God had really worked everything out in the most creative way possible. In fact, I began to wonder if maybe God had caused the fire, since it had occurred within an hour of my giving everything back to him.

By December, everything was paid off, and the weight of the debt was lifted. We had equity in our home again, and we were able to move back in. Without the noose of unpaid bills hanging around my neck, I wondered if maybe I could fulfill a longtime desire of mine. For years, I had wanted to go to Bible college to dive deeper into the Bible and become more effective in ministering to others. But with a family and a failing business, there was no way I could have even considered it before. It was a dream I had buried, feeling like the burden of my debt was hindering me from what God was calling me to do.

Obviously, I still had to provide for my family's daily needs. I asked God to make it crystal clear.

"If you want me to go to Bible college, please open the door, and I will walk through it."

Over the next three weeks, I was able to complete projects and made $20,000 — enough for my family to live on for four months, as well as pay for the first term of school.

Over the next two years, I grew tremendously in my relationship with God and loved every single minute of Bible school. Each semester, I was amazed that God provided the exact amount of money we needed right before classes began, often in miraculous ways. I had no doubt that I was exactly where I was supposed to be.

❧ ❧ ❧

I finished school December 13, 2012. On January 1, I sat my family down. "The last two years have been about me pursuing Bible college," I began. "This next year, what do you guys want to do?"

I had called a family meeting, and now I waited eagerly for their responses. I had a feeling what they would want, and I glanced around at my children's beautiful faces, from my oldest to my youngest.

"Well, I'd like to do more fishing and hunting," Tyler suggested hesitantly.

"Yes, me, too!" Jack agreed.

"I'd like to do more outdoor stuff together as a family," Chloe offered.

Hannah nodded her agreement. "I want to ride horses more."

"Well, good! It's settled. Outdoor stuff it is! What would you guys think if we moved to Eastern Oregon or somewhere like that?"

A chorus of cheers erupted from the couch. We had always loved our camping and horse-packing expeditions out that direction.

Tina's eyes met mine, and she gave me a sheepish grin.

"Do you think we could get into a house that's not falling apart?" Her eyes sparkled.

I laughed. "Let me see what we can do."

The summer of 2013, I accepted a job as a park ranger.

We joined Harvest Church in Baker City and began an overall different lifestyle from what we had been used to. During our first year in Eastern Oregon, we moved three times before God provided the perfect home for our family. Not just a house but a beautiful log home with a shop fully supplied with tools. We grew closer as a family and spent more time together. If we'd learned anything from our days in the camper, it was that it's not a house that makes a home.

No matter where we went, whether at the local swimming pool or the grocery store or even at my job, it seemed like God was always putting people who needed him in my path. And wherever I was, I did what I felt he was telling me to do. People needed to know about Jesus, and I finally felt adequately prepared to share the good news with them.

～～～

"I can't believe they just *gave* these snowmobiles to us!" Tyler said, gushing in his excitement.

"I know. It's especially cool because we sold ours years ago," I answered, pulling my ski cap tightly around my head. "It's like God's paying us back a little bit. He just does stuff like that sometimes."

Tina and the younger kids were loading up into their snowmobiles, too, ready for a day of exploring the lovely winter landscape before us.

"You guys ready?" Hannah called out.

"You bet!" I yelled back, and we were off. True joy and love for my family surged through my body.

As we headed into the Oregon wilderness, witnessing the vast creation surrounding me, it was crazy to think about how much had to happen for God to get me to that point.

I had to be completely broken, and I had to learn to trust him completely. It seems God had to drag us through a knothole for us to see any heavenly good sometimes. My story was far from over, and I knew there was much more for God to do in my life and through me. But at last I had crossed over and learned to trust God with everything. I no longer equated material goods with success. We didn't have a lot of money, but our needs were met, and we knew we were precisely where we were supposed to be.

CONCLUSION

My heart is full. When I became a pastor, my desire was to change the world. My hope was to see people encouraged and the hurting filled with hope. As I read this book, I saw that passion being fulfilled. However, at Harvest Church, rather than being content with our past victories, we are spurred to believe that many more can occur. Every time we see another changed life, it increases our awareness that God really loves people and he is actively seeking to change lives. Think about it: How did you get this book? We believe you read this book because God brought it to you seeking to reveal his love to you. Whether you're a man or a woman, a farmer or a waitress, blue collar or no collar, a parent or a student, a teacher or park ranger, we believe God came to save you. He came to save all of us from the hellish pain we've wallowed in and offer real joy and the opportunity to share in real life that will last forever through faith in Jesus Christ.

Do you have honest questions that such radical change is possible? It seems too good to be true, doesn't it? Each of us at Harvest Church warmly invites you to come and check out our church family. Freely ask questions, examine our statements, see if we're "for real" and, if you choose, journey with us at whatever pace you are comfortable. You will find that we are far from perfect. Our scars and sometimes open wounds are still healing, but we just want you to know God is still completing the process of authentic life change in us. We still make mistakes in our journey, like everyone will. Therefore, we acknowledge our continued need for each other's forgiveness and support. We need the love of God just as much as we did the day before we believed in him.

If you are unable to be with us, yet you intuitively sense you would really like to experience such a life change, here are some basic thoughts to consider. If you choose, at the end of this conclusion, you can pray the suggested prayer. If your prayer genuinely comes from your heart, you will experience the beginning stages of authentic life change, similar to those you have read about.

How does this change occur?

Recognize that what you're doing isn't working. Accept the fact that Jesus desires to forgive you for your bad decisions and selfish motives. Realize that without this forgiveness, you will continue a life separated from God and his amazing love. In the Bible, the book of Romans, chapter 6, verse 23 tells us that the result of sin (seeking our way rather than God's way) is death, but the gift that God freely gives is everlasting life found in Jesus Christ.

Believe in your heart that God passionately loves you and wants to give you a new heart. Ezekiel 11:19 reads, "I will give them singleness of heart and put a new spirit within them. I will take away their stony, stubborn heart and give them a tender, responsive heart" (NLT).

CONCLUSION

Believe in your heart that "if you confess with your mouth that Jesus is Lord and believe in your heart that God raised him from the dead, you will be saved" (Romans 10:9 NLT).

Believe in your heart that because Jesus paid for your failure and wrong motives, and because you asked him to forgive you, he has filled your new heart with his life in such a way that he transforms you from the inside out. Second Corinthians 5:17 reads, "When someone becomes a Christian, he becomes a brand new person inside. He is not the same anymore. A new life has begun!"

Why not pray now?

Lord Jesus, if I've learned one thing in my journey, it's that you are God and I am not. My choices have not resulted in the happiness I hoped they would bring. Not only have I experienced pain, I've also caused it. I know I am separated from you, but I want that to change. I am sorry for the choices I've made that have hurt myself, others and denied you. I believe your death paid for my sins, and you are now alive to change me from the inside out. Would you please do that now? I ask you to come and live in me so that I can sense you are here with me. Thank you for hearing and changing me. Now please help me know when you are talking to me, so I can cooperate with your efforts to change me. Amen.

Baker City's unfolding story of God's love is still being written — and your name is in it. I hope to see you this Sunday!

Pastor Brad Phillips
Harvest Church
Baker City, Oregon

We would love for you to join us at Harvest Church!

We meet Sunday mornings at 10:10 a.m. at
3720 Birch Street, Baker City, OR 97814.

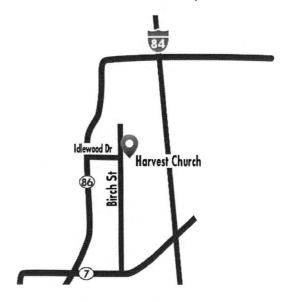

Contact Information
Phone: 541.523.4233
Web site: www.bakercityharvest.org
Email: admin@bakercityharvest.org

Other Service Times
Sunday: Harvest Café at 9 a.m.
Sunday: Youth Group at 6 p.m.
Wednesday: Children/Youth Gatherings at 6:30 p.m.

For more information on reaching your city with stories from your church, go to www.testimonybooks.com.

GOOD CATCH
PUBLISHING